WILEY G. HAINES

FRONTIER U.S. DEPUTY MARSHAL

J. D. HAINES, M.D.

EAKIN PRESS ◆ Fort Worth, Texas
www.EakinPress.com

For my mother and father

CONTENTS

FOREWORD

Forty years ago I spent parts of two summers examining the contents of a pair of large trunks stored in the attic of my grandparents' home. The trunks contained letters, official documents, photographs, cards, wanted posters, newspapers, journals, and all sorts of information pertaining to life in frontier Indian Territory. From these primary sources my son, Joe Jr., and I began piecing together the life story of U.S. Deputy Marshal Wiley G. Haines. The picture of a remarkable man emerged, and it is his story that we have sought to preserve.

Haines' ancestors were Quakers who journeyed from Northampton, England, in 1682, to the New World. The Quakers were at the forefront of protecting the rights of Native Americans. In this tradition, Haines also served the Native American people with distinction. Most importantly, here was a white man whom the Indians could trust. The protection of the Osage Tribe was more than just a professional responsibility, however.

Haines learned the Osage language and became a trusted friend of the tribe. He made numerous trips to Washington, representing the Osages on official business with the Department of Interior. After witnessing the injustices suffered by Native Americans, it must have given Haines particular pleasure to see the Osages become the wealthiest people per capita on earth, thanks to oil royalties.

The true measure of a lawman was not the number of outlaws he killed, although Haines' pistol contains six notches, but how effectively he kept the peace. The assignment as a federal officer in Indian Territory was one of the most difficult in the country. Most of the officers performed their duties without fanfare or recognition. Lawmen like Wiley Haines, Bud Ledbetter, Charlie Colcord, Frank Canton, Warren Bennett, Bass Reeves, and others were the iron men of the era. They were true professionals and far removed from the Hollywood version of lawmen.

For nearly thirty years Wiley Haines held a commission as a U.S. deputy marshal. He protected not only the people, but the land as well, as an early conservationist. Several writers have referred to him as the "Peacemaker of the Osage."

It is difficult for us today to conceive of the hardships that Haines dealt with on a daily basis. Whether riding on horseback through the snow in bitter cold pursuing an outlaw or facing the guns of desperadoes, Haines had to be prepared for anything.

The United States Marshals Foundation has written, "For 200 years these lawmen remained the least known to the public except for the legends created around a handful of individuals who helped tame the West; Bat Masterson, Wild Bill Hickok, and Wyatt Earp for example.

"Earp served less than six months, Masterson wore a deputy's badge, not out West but in New York City. Hickok worked as a deputy before wanderlust lured him farther West."

Unlike these high-profile lawmen that Western writers love so well, Haines was a career lawman. Hill's *History of the State of Oklahoma*, published in 1909, said this about Wiley Haines:

"In reviewing the salient points which mark the career of Wiley G. Haines it is found that he has won the reputation of being one of the most successful criminal officers in Oklahoma, earnest and fearless in the discharge of his duties in various official positions, including those of U.S. Deputy Marshal, Chief of Police for the Osage nation and for several years criminal officer of enviable record in Oklahoma."

Before Haines died at sixty-eight, he could take satisfaction in seeing a wild and lawless frontier take its place in civilized society. His funeral was the largest his hometown had ever seen. He touched lives as a cowboy, educator, lawman, rancher, school board member, Thirty-second-degree Mason, father, and friend. The epitaph on his tombstone sums up his life:

"An Honest Man's the Noblest Work of God."

Here is the story of Wiley G. Haines.

—JOE D. HAINES, SR.

CHAPTER I

THE MAN AND THE LEGEND

The peace officer of the American West is best known by the popular myths that have become indistinguishable from historical fact. Historians are quick to dismantle the fantastic distortions produced by dime novelists and pulp fiction writers. The exploits of real characters such as Wild Bill Hickok and Wyatt Earp were exaggerated to such an extent that the accomplishments of real officers are often discounted.

Today the pendulum has swung too far in the other direction. The current representation of the western peace officer as an ordinary citizen carrying out routine duties is not an entirely accurate portrayal, either. In Oklahoma and Indian Territories during the 1890s and early 1900s, there was nothing ordinary about the demands on law enforcement officers. The men who stepped forward as federal marshals were the real stuff of legend.

On the frontier that we now know as Oklahoma, federal marshals took the most notable roles in the American West. The territory, which had been reserved for relocated Indian tribes from all over the country, fell under the jurisdiction of the federal court for western Arkansas. By 1889 the growing population and general condition of lawlessness led to the division of the area into two enormous districts, Oklahoma and Indian Territories.

By the turn of the century, the territories had earned a reputation as a refuge for every sort of outlaw. Fugitives from surround-

ing states could escape into the territories, where they could be ex-
tradited only for federal offenses. U.S. Marshal Wiley G. Haines described the times as follows:

"The country was teeming with horse thieves, whiskey peddlers
and every sort of fugitive. The officers' job was often made difficult
by the lack of help provided by the citizens who were cowed by the
outlaws."[1]

Chris Madsen, longtime marshal, described the era similarly:

"The opening of the country to settlement and the closing of
many of the large cattle pastures, left a number of the cowboys out
of employment. They had been used to the free and roaming life on
the open prairie, and they could not content themselves to be confined to a farm half a mile square. They took up other vocations,
principally peddling whiskey to Indians, rustling cattle, robbing
trains and banks..."[2]

The land runs attracted a wide cross-section of personalities,
from the adventurous and courageous, to the wild and foolhardy, to
the maladjusted and sociopathic. Add to this mix the assorted fugitives and criminals, and a handful of federal law enforcement officers to keep the peace, and the situation could be conservatively described as volatile.

Oklahoma and Indian Territory quickly became the most chal-
lenging post in the nation for a federal marshal. It was here that the
legends are based in fact. No myths or fictitious embellishments were
needed to enhance the accomplishments of men like Wiley Haines.

Sometimes Haines' job turned violent, as illustrated by the six
notches carved into his .44 caliber Colt revolver. The six notches
represent the six outlaws who challenged the wrong lawman and
paid with their lives.

For thirty-eight years Wiley served as a peace officer. When he
died in 1928, an era in frontier law enforcement ended. The *Tulsa
World* best eulogized his passing:

> There was in the time of Haines, Bud Ledbetter and Frank
> Canton no elaborate law organization. An officer then was literally
> the law and nothing but his judgment and his trigger finger stood be-
> tween him and extermination. He had nowhere to pass the buck, no
> alibi, no reinforcements. It was often the case of a lone man against
> a pack of cunning devils long used to the brush and the cave. These

men of law had no brass bands, typewriter or press agents and they had to be deadly as rattlesnakes.

Haines, like most of the real officers of his time, was rather modest and unpretentious. Practically none of the old-time officers, with the exception of Heck Thomas, had the courtly manner, the dramatic look or the towering presence. They were the forerunners of out civilization and their job was a grim one. They were just as far from the movie type of gunfighter as possible. They were direct representatives of the United States and they acted directly.

The passing of these unromantic men constitutes the passing of an era. It was a rough and ugly era, but in the light of that which came after, it was heroic and exciting.[3]

CHAPTER II

EARLY YEARS

The fall of 1860 was one of the most turbulent times in American history. The nation, not yet one hundred years old, was facing a crisis. The differences between the North and South were proving truly irreconcilable.

Into this chaotic time a baby was born on October 7, 1860, to the Reverend John Williamson Haines and his wife, Mary Elizabeth. The family lived in Monroe County, Missouri, where Reverend Haines ministered to his Baptist congregation and operated a farm. The baby was John and Mary's second child, and they named him Wiley Green.

Young Wiley was just a day shy of being one month old when Abraham Lincoln was elected the sixteenth president of the United States. Lincoln's election worsened the situation in the southern states; tempers quickened and concerns increased. The day following Lincoln's election, November 7, 1860, South Carolina became the first state to threaten secession. In Charleston, the palmetto flag was raised in defiance of Lincoln's election.

The newly organized Kansas Territory, on Missouri's western border, attracted more and more antislavery settlers. Missouri feared that Kansas would be admitted as a free state, and as a result conflicts broke out between Kansans and Missourians.

South Carolina became the first state to secede from the Union, on December 20, 1860. By the spring of 1861, ten other states had joined South Carolina to form the Confederate States of America. Missouri then became the center of attention as everyone wondered whether Missouri would secede or remain with the Union.

When President Lincoln called for troops from Missouri to help fill the ranks of the federal army, the pro-Southern governor refused. The Missouri State Guard, commanded by Major General Sterling Price, clashed with the Federal Army at Booneville, Missouri, in June of that year.

The Federals were commanded by newly minted Brigadier General Nathaniel Lyon. Lyon routed the militiamen and gained control of northern Missouri. In the process, Lyon's men killed a number of civilians. The militia retreated to southwestern Missouri and reorganized with regular Confederate troops under Brigadier General Benjamin McCulloch.

The impetuous General Lyon marched his little army to southwestern Missouri with the goal of ridding the state of all armed Confederates. Against his better judgement, Lyon allowed himself to be talked into an attack by one of his officers, Franz Sigel. On August 10, 1861, at Wilson's Creek, near Springfield, Lyon attacked the Confederate army. Lyon was killed in the battle, and his army was forced to retreat, leaving southwestern Missouri in Confederate hands.

Throughout the Civil War, bands of both Union and Confederate guerrillas terrorized the Missouri countryside. Towns were burned and looted, and these marauding bands murdered many innocent people.

William A. Settle characterized the era well in his book about the life of Jesse James:

> Nothing has ever been witnessed in American life like the horror, terrorism, bloodshed and disregard for human life that Southern guerrillas wreaked upon large areas of Missouri between the fall of 1861 and the spring of 1865. Since Federal troops in the area were also guilty of acts of unbelievable brutality, residents of the state endured the worst of an irregular war from both sides.
>
> Interference with unoffending citizens, arbitrary arrest and imprisonment of men and women, illegal requisitioning of supplies by irresponsible citizens, robbery, pillage, arson and murder by Federal and state troops created an environment conducive to the most desperate measures of reprisal.[1]

William Francis Haines, Wiley's uncle, was a Missouri farmer who wrote down his recollections of the war in 1916. Even though W. F. Haines admitted, "I was in the last of the war and never in a regular battle," his writings paint a vivid picture of how the war affected civilians as well as soldiers. He served with his county militia in the early part of the war and was an officer with the 42nd Regiment of the Missouri Volunteer Infantry.

"We had a hard time to live at all," W. F. Haines recalled of the war years:

> We would go to the mill 25 or 30 miles away and get 5 or 6 bushels of corn meal and the Rebel soldiers would help us eat it up. Soon they took all the mills to grind for soldiers. When General Lions [Lyon] was killed at Wilson's Creek near Springfield, Missouri, I was 8 miles west of there on my way to Bowers mill on Spring River, with ten bushels of wheat, the blind horse and a colt 14 months old. I heard the cannon roaring for two hours or more. I was lucky to get home with my flour in 8 days. After I got back with it, from 6 to 8 soldiers [came] every day till it was gone....
>
> We had to live on roasting ears and potatoes 2 weeks, before corn got hard enough to grit on a tin grater, then we done fine. Oh, how I would have liked to have found a large M.J.B. coffee can or baking powder can to make a gritter out of. It was quite a job to make meal for 10 of us, but it was good bread with plenty [of] eggs in it. That is how we got our bread until the third day of Dec. 1861.[2]

The state of Missouri was split, with two separate governments and representation in both the U.S. Congress and the Confederate Congress. There was much bitterness in the state due to Lyon's high-handed tactics. Missouri was plagued for the duration of the war by vicious partisan warfare. Federal forces defeated the Confederates on March 7–8, 1862, at the Battle of Pea Ridge in northern Arkansas and gained control of Missouri for the Union.

In Monroe County, a gang of outlaws, contemptuously known as "the home guard," roamed the countryside looting and pillaging. When the citizens had finally had enough, they rose up in defiance of the gang's depredations. In response, the home guard secreted away one of their members and claimed that the protesting citizens had killed him.

Thirty falsely accused men were rounded up and arrested by the

Union Army for the "murder." The Reverend Haines and a brother were among the thirty scapegoats. The prisoners were transported to a federal prison in Illinois. Biographical information supplied by John Haines indicated that he and his brother escaped from a federal prison in Quincy, Illinois. However, no historical records exist indicating that there was a prison in Quincy. There did exist an infamous military prison in nearby Alton, Illinois. It is possible that Quincy was a layover for the prisoners en route to Alton, and Reverend Haines and his brother escaped there. Or perhaps the records were incorrect, and the Haines brothers were actually imprisoned at Alton.

Reverend Haines reported that ten of the thirty were executed by firing squad. The odds for prisoners at Alton were not much better. Disease raged, largely due to the deplorable conditions, overcrowding, and inadequate medical treatment. Diarrhea and pneumonia killed many men, but smallpox was the most dreaded disease. The epidemic resulted in a smallpox hospital being established on a small island in the Mississippi River near the prison. For many men, incarceration at the Alton Military Prison was in effect a death sentence.[3]

Seeing that their best chance for survival lay in escape, Haines and his brother made a daring breakout and found their way home. In the meantime, the home guard was preying upon the families of the thirty men. One day, two members of the home guard appeared at the Haines home, pulled their guns, and demanded money from Mary Haines. She stood her ground and flatly refused. The pair responded that they would "blow her brains out" if she didn't hand over the money. But Mary was not to be intimidated by two lowly cowards. She looked them in the eye and calmly responded, "If men are so small as to murder women for a little bit of money, I would rather not live!"[4]

The men realized that they had been bested and halfheartedly threatened to abduct little Wiley, but they were cowed by Mary's brave defiance and rode away empty-handed. At the end of Wiley's life, many would admire his courageous exploits, but few know of the brave role models he had in his parents.

Wiley Haines descended from a long line of adventurous ancestors, including Richard Haines, a Quaker who had immigrated to the colonies from England in 1682. Richard was related to Simeon Heynes, one of the revisers of the Liturgy of the Episcopal Church, eighth president of Queens College, Cambridge, vice chancellor of the University, and Henry VIII's Minister to France.

Richard died during the voyage to the New World on the ship *Amity*, and his wife Margaret bore a son, Joseph, before the ship arrived. The family settled in West Jersey, and the branch that descended to Wiley Haines' family settled in Virginia.[5]

Although raised a Methodist, Wiley's father, John, became a Baptist and attended seminary in Palmyra, Missouri. He was licensed as a preacher in 1854 and ordained in 1860.[6]

When the tragic chapter of the Civil War finally ended, the country began the painful process of reconstruction. The hard times had taken a toll on Mary Haines' health. She was advised by her physicians to seek a more healthful climate in the West, so the family made plans to move. Shortly after they set out, reports of Indian attacks on the western plains forced them to turn back to Lawrence County, Missouri.

But the stress of the journey proved too much for Mary, and she died in Lawrence County. The family resettled in Cedar County, Missouri, where Wiley, now thirteen, managed the family farm while his father preached. Farming, however, was not a life that held much interest for the boy. By the time he was fifteen, in 1876, Wiley convinced his father that he was ready to set out on a great adventure—his first cattle drive.

CHAPTER III

COWBOY

In 1876 the most exciting adventure a young man could imagine was a western trail drive. Wiley's first real job away from home was helping to drive 150 head of cattle from Missouri to Fort Verde, Arizona.

A typical trail herd could cover twelve to sixteen miles per day before bedding the cattle down at night. But even at night, someone had to remain alert in case the cattle became "spooked" or "boogered" and a stampede resulted. One can only imagine the adventure of sleeping out every night under the stars, sitting around the campfire, and living a life others could only dream of.

Somewhere along the way, Wiley purchased his first pistol and practiced until he developed speed and accuracy. One hundred thirty-seven days after they began, the trail drive ended in Fort Verde. Wiley arrived with five cents in his pocket and a wealth of experience. He decided to try his hand at cowboying and worked on ranches in Arizona for the next two years.

In an interview given just six months before his death in 1928, Wiley compared himself to a character in a 1922 novel by Emerson Hough, *The Covered Wagon*. The story tells of the wagon train journey of hardy pioneers from Missouri to Oregon in 1848. Wiley recalled, "The story... could easily be a story of our westward trip. I might have been the freckle-faced pioneer lad in the famous story."[1]

Wiley eventually grew homesick for the green hills of Missouri and signed on with an eastward-bound wagon train. The hardest part of the journey was crossing the mountains. Concern arose when it was learned that the Apache warrior Victorio was terrorizing the area the wagon train was about to cross. A meeting was convened to discuss whether the wagon train should turn back. Victorio was feared as a formidable warrior.

Victorio spent his early years as a warrior under Mangas Colorado and also alongside Cochise's Chiricahuas before becoming a Mimbreno chief. In the spring of 1877, after nearly seventeen years of intermittent warfare with the white man, Victorio's band settled in southwestern New Mexico. The reservation contained their favorite campsite, *Ojo Caliente,* which seemed to content the tribe. But in the spring of 1879, the U.S. government transferred the band to the poor San Carlos Reservation in southeastern Arizona.

Refusing to accept this unwise decision, Victorio fled to Texas with thirty braves and was joined by eighty Mescaleros. In September of 1879, he led his warriors north and attacked a company of the Ninth U.S. Cavalry camping near *Ojo Caliente.* The Apaches killed eight troopers and stole over forty horses. Over the next several weeks, the Apaches killed eighteen more white men before disappearing into Mexico. For months, Victorio's band continued making raids into western Texas and New Mexico.

Fears of Victorio were well justified. After much heated discussion among the members of the wagon train, a vote was finally taken. When all had voted except Wiley, the count was evenly split. Half wanted to go on, half wanted to turn back. Everyone turned to Wiley to see how he would cast the deciding vote. Wiley never hesitated. They would continue on.

The wagon train took extra precautions for a possible attack by fortifying their camps each night, but Victorio's band never materialized. The wagon train completed its journey in 100 days.

When he returned to Missouri, Wiley found his father working hard to help establish Southwest Baptist College in Missouri. The school was located in Bolivar, and Wiley enrolled, completed his education, and remained as a teacher until 1886. His father taught German and served as an administrator for the school. At one time, Reverend Haines was offered the presidency of the college, but he declined for health reasons.

In 1886 Wiley again headed west, this time with his sights on

California. Not a great deal is known of Wiley's life in California, other than he became interested in a medical career and worked as an apprentice for a Dr. Long. For a time, he also worked for a street-car line. While in California, Wiley received several letters from his father requesting help in raising funds for the financially strapped college. One letter, dated June 20, 1888, read as follows:

> Wiley, My Son, I want to talk to you specially about our College. While I believe in special providence, Yet I believe in special means to bring about events. One of the great events, most to be deplored by us at the present time would be the collapse of our College. The greatest event in our estimation would be the liquidation, or payment of all these liabilities. The impression is forcing help upon us that unless aid shall be given by Sep. that the College and grounds will be sold to satisfy the claim of Wilson and Thom, for $3,000. Now, it is a distant hope, but is there not some noble, liberal-hearted man in the bounds of the Golden State of California that would come to the rescue of our cherished institution and save it to the denomination and to future generations? Could you find yourself inquiring in a quiet way of public-spirited persons and ascertain, who amongst them would be likely to aid a worthy cause?
>
> I hear there are a great many millionaires in California and no doubt there are a great many who are not so rich who are nevertheless as willing if the right influence was brought to bear on them.

The Reverend Haines, who was a published poet, closed this letter to Wiley with the following verse:

> "You and I, can only try.
> If we ask the Lord, we have His word.
> If agreed in the request, and He thinks it best,
> 'Tis to Him no task, and we shall have what we ask."[2]

There is no record of Wiley finding a benevolent millionaire, but the college managed to survive. Wiley's stay in California ended when he learned of the opening of the Unassigned Lands in Oklahoma in 1889. At twenty-nine he was still single, well educated, and eager to participate in one of the greatest adventures of the decade. When the bugles sounded and the shotgun blasts exploded at noon on April 22, 1889, Wiley was on the first train into the territory.

CHAPTER IV

LAND RUN

The American West held such vast reserves of land in the 1800s that its availability to settlers seemed unlimited. But by 1889, much of the desirable land in the West had been occupied. Many homesteaders had their eyes on the Unassigned Lands in Oklahoma. David Payne, the leader of a group known as the Boomers, popularized removing the barriers to the settlement of the territory. The Boomers advocated immediate settlement of the Unassigned Lands and in numerous cases staked claims before the government had opened the land to settlement.

The Boomer cause won support in Congress, leading to the attachment of a rider to the Indian Appropriation Bill (the Springer Amendment), which provided for the opening of the Unassigned Lands. President Benjamin Harrison issued a proclamation declaring the Unassigned Lands open for settlement on April 22, 1889.

The Unassigned Lands accounted for about two million acres, which meant that a limited number of claims were available. To provide a fair opportunity for all who sought land, a land run was organized. For three days prior to the land run, settlers would be allowed to assemble on the four borders of the Unassigned Lands awaiting the starting signal. The four-week period between President Harrison's proclamation and the actual opening was intended to give people time to reach the territory. But it also gave them plenty of time to scheme.

For the previous ten years, Boomers had hoped that their incursions into the Unassigned Lands would be legally recognized, as had occurred elsewhere in the West. "Squatter's rights" had been invoked in the past to initiate property claims.

But this was not to occur in Oklahoma. Those who had previously entered the Unassigned Lands early in defiance of the proclamation became known as "Sooners." These Sooners had already staked claims before those in compliance with the law had even set out.

A settler's claim had to be registered at a land office, and disputes between claimants arose almost immediately. Many of the disputes were settled in court, but many ended in violence.

Government officials anticipated around 5,000 people showing up for the free land, but over 50,000 materialized to make the run.

The federal government had also neglected to provide for any organized territorial government, so the people took matters into their own hands. As Dr. Delos Walker later wrote,

"The denizens of all civilization came; came from the hills, from the caves of the earth, from the isles of the sea and, seemingly, from the clouds of air. They were here in all tongues, in all colors, in all garbs, with all kinds of profanity and every imaginable odor; were here at high noon."[1]

Wiley Haines was among this throng and decided that rail was the best way to reach Oklahoma Station, where he wanted to stake his claim. Oklahoma Station would be transformed overnight into Oklahoma City. The new Santa Fe line from Arkansas City, Kansas, which had been built to join the Gulf track from Galveston, passed through the Oklahoma Station. The line had been opened just twenty-two months before the land run.

For the opening, the Santa Fe assembled all the spare equipment it could muster. Eleven trains ran from the north, carrying 1,000 people each. The Gulf line sent up six trains, also filled to capacity. On April 22, the southbound trains from Arkansas City were halted at Orlando, north of the border, about fifty miles from Oklahoma Station and twenty miles north of the Cimarron River.

The northbound train, from Texas, was also held at Purcell, on the South Canadian, thirty-three miles south of Oklahoma Station.[2] It was in Purcell that Wiley boarded the train.

When the army bugle sounded at noon and shots exploded into the clear blue sky, a stampede ensued such as the country had never witnessed. At 2:05 P.M., the crowded Santa Fe train that Haines was aboard pulled into Oklahoma Station, and the hundreds of passengers descended. Some crawled through the train windows rather than wait. People with stakes and hammers in their hands ran about frantically, trying to stake a lot.

At 3:00 P.M. the Santa Fa train from Kansas pulled in, and the scene was repeated. Some 6,000 people slept on the prairie that night, and by the next morning two more trains had brought in hundreds more settlers to add to those arriving by buggy, by wagon, and by foot. One week later, around one thousand buildings had been hastily erected.

By May 6, a provisional government was in place, but it relied on the military to preserve order. Captain D. F. Stiles of the U.S. Army Tenth Infantry was the acting executive officer and provost marshal. His troopers patrolled the grounds of the "city." An idea of the conditions can be had from reading *Oklahoma City Times* reporter Robe Carl White's description:

> It was common to see men with ammunition belts strapped around their waists with one or two .45s in their holsters... many carrying rifles. Main Street (the principal business section) was the dividing line. The main residential district was located on the highlands extending north. The honkytonk district, dance halls, cribs, and dives were mostly on the north side. Gambling houses centered on the streets fronting the railroad and depot and extended south four or five blocks and were called "Gamblers' Row." Every kind of gambling could be found on the "Row." Street fakirs, medicine shows and con men filled the open space in front....
>
> This section of town was crowded night and day... it was a feverish atmosphere and excitement ran high. The majority had nothing to do except hold down their lots; it is no wonder that games of chance attracted great crowds. A dog fight in a street would attract a huge crowd within a few minutes, to say nothing about fights, gun fights... arguments of all kinds.[3]

Another apt description of the beginnings of Oklahoma City came from Colonel D. F. MacMartin's book *Thirty Years in Hell*:

> History has never recorded an opening of government land whereon there was assembled such a rash and motley colony of gam-

blers, cut-throats, refugees, demimondaines, bootleggers and high
hat and low-pressure crooks... The spectacular array included the
Kansas Jayhawker, the Arkansas Reuben Glue, shaking with the
buck ague; the Missouri puke, the Texas ranger, the Illinois sucker,
et. al. There were nesters, horse thieves, train robbers, hijackers, bank
raiders, yeggmen, ragamuffins and vagabonds, brand blotters, broncho
busters, sheep herders, cow punchers, spoofers, bull whackers, range
riders, minute jacks, wildcatters, fourflushers, Chevalrie d'industrie,
outlanders, montebanks, confidence men, sand lotters and proletari-
ats, sun-chasers, blown-up suckers, fire-eaters, tenderfeet, land
whales, butterfly chasers, blue-sky promoters, sour-doughs, ticket-of-
leavers, fellows with nicked reputations, geezers who had just been lib-
erated from the hulks and had ugly corners of their lives to live
down... There was Piute Charley, Cold Deck Mike, Alibi Pete,
Alkali Ike, Comanche Hank, False Alarm Andy, Poker Jim,
Rattlesnake Jack, Six-shooter Bill and Cactus Sam.

Not one to fear risking hyperbole, MacMartin continues,

There were marksmen who were quick on the draw and could
throw a half dollar in the air and clip it with a bullet from their revolvers three times out of five... Among these prospective settlers
were ancient maidens, fainting Berthas, wappened widows, withered
amazons. There were scoundrels and camouflage artists-bastard
scum of the earth and spawn of the devil who would not scruple to
take unfair opportunities of their next door neighbors, glib and slippery creatures, together with a homogenous smear of other short-
horns... offscourings and human birds of passage in every stage of
shipwrecked penury.... Some of these settlers had left families,
creditors and in a paucity of instances even officers of justice, per-
plexed and lamenting. Some had deserted their wives for the wives of
others, for this sanctuary. It is no grotesque assertion to say that
some of the best men had the worst antecedents, some of the worst
rejoiced in spotless, puritan pedigrees.[4]

The town was quickly overrun with "lot jumpers," who sought
out the claims of those known to be Sooners. They would come in
force and oust the owner, taking possession of his claim. Often the
confrontation turned violent.

On a bigger scale, 250 men tried to jump a claim defended by
ten men. The army troops arrived just in time to prevent a bloody

showdown. Another group of 500 men raided a claim on the west side of the city but were run out by Captain Stiles and his men.

The job of a law-enforcement officer in Oklahoma City became one of the toughest assignments in the country. A survival-of-the-fittest mentality prevailed, and city fathers wisely organized a police force. As author Glenn Shirley relates in his book *West of Hell's Fringe*:

> The first brick building, situated in the heart of the city, boasted a liquor store on the first floor, police headquarters and police court on the second, and a jail in the basement. At the front door of this building, Sheriff John Fightmaster killed Scarface Joe, an Indian who tried to flee from his cell. Dr. I.W. Folsom, a physician from the Choctaw Nation and the Democratic nominee for mayor, got off to a bad start by trying to kill saloonkeeper Phil Rogers with a Mexican bowie knife. U.S. Deputy Marshal Charles F. Colcord bounced the barrel of his six-shooter off Folsom's head in time to save Roger's life.[5]

In the midst of this turmoil, Haines managed to stake his claim and soon joined Charles F. Colcord in the real-estate business. In the confusion and chaos, many people staked claims that were already occupied, or they were simply too slow in finding a lot. Such was the fate of a widow and her family, who were unsuccessful in their attempt to secure a lot. In a gesture of extraordinary generosity, Haines voluntarily relinquished his claim to the unknown widow.[6]

As fate would have it, the magnanimous gesture probably cost Haines a fortune. His real-estate partner, Charles F. Colcord, went on to make millions in real estate and became one of the wealthiest men in Oklahoma City. If Haines had regrets, however, he never admitted them. He and Colcord remained close friends all their lives. Haines had a standing invitation at the Colcord mansion whenever he was in Oklahoma City on business.

One day in 1890, when the city was about a year old, Haines chanced to be conversing with a group of men that included Captain C. H. DeFord. DeFord had been elected the first sheriff of Oklahoma City and was looking for men to guard some prisoners. One of the men in the group knew Haines and volunteered that he was a dependable, honest man. DeFord offered Haines a job on the spot. Haines accepted, was made a deputy sheriff, and embarked on a thirty-eight-year career in law enforcement.

Sheriff DeFord presented Wiley with his first service revolver, an

1876 model Colt .44 caliber revolver. The backstrap of the pistol was inscribed, "Wiley G. Haines from C. H. DeFord." Haines quickly earned a reputation as a trustworthy and competent officer. He liked the work well enough to remain on as a deputy for DeFord's successor, his old friend Charles Colcord.

Colcord's family was originally from Kentucky, and he worked as a rancher until the land run in 1889. Colcord was appointed the first chief of police of Oklahoma City and was elected sheriff in late 1890, serving a two-year term. Following his term, he was appointed the U.S. deputy marshal in charge of Oklahoma City by U.S. Marshal E. D. Nix.

Colcord later commented in his autobiography, "The deputies serving under me in the district were a fine bunch of officers and as brave men as ever lived. Frank N. Canton, Bill Tilghman, Ike Steel, Frank Lake, George Mouser, Wiley Haines, George Stormer, Henry Callahan, Morris Robecker and Ed Stagy were some of these brave fellows."[7]

While working in Oklahoma City, Haines met a young woman named Sarah Tapp. Sarah was living with a sister-in-law, Katie Woodruff, who was proving up on a claim she had staked in Oklahoma City. Sarah was from Brown County, Illinois, the daughter of farmers John and Mary Tapp.

Sarah and Wiley fell in love and married in Oklahoma City on January 27, 1892. The bride was twenty years old and the groom ten years her senior. The young couple remained only a short time in the city before moving north for the opening of the Cherokee Outlet the following year.

As in the previous opening of the Unassigned Lands, towns sprang up within hours. Some 25,000 people settled in and around Perry. "The city appeared stretched all over the face of the earth, an inextricable mix-up of horses, mules and equipage... a half dozen people seemed to be holding down each lot."[8]

The *Guthrie Daily News* of September 20, 1893, described the scene in graphic detail: "Sand covered everything; the dust created from the tramp of hoofs and human feet rendered the air unbearable to a degree of suffocation. Drinking water, hauled in tanks on carts, sold at five cents a glass; water fit for livestock was almost unobtainable; and bathing was out of the question. Tents, dugouts, hoisted wagon tongues draped with canvas, and other crude shelters were being erected by the light of flaming torches. Business establishments were beehives of activity, and around the temporary saloons was pandemonium."[9]

Seven new counties were added to Oklahoma Territory following the Cherokee Outlet Run and were designated Counties K, L, M, N, O, P, and Q. County P was subsequently named Noble County, with its county seat at Perry.

Wiley and Sarah moved to a farm near Perry, where Haines worked as undersheriff for Sheriff J. C. Scruggs of County P. Perry quickly acquired the reputation of being so tough that a section of town became known as Hell's Half Acre. The territorial governor received so many complaints of robberies and homicides in the gambling district that raids were conducted and the gambling dens closed.

The government's plans to prevent the problems with the Unassigned Land run failed miserably. Thousands of Sooners had again managed to enter the restricted area before the appointed hour on September 16, 1893. Eight million acres and approximately 100,000 new citizens were added to Oklahoma Territory in one afternoon.

The site reserved for the Perry townsite proved much too small, and a North Perry, West Perry, and South Perry (Wharton) quickly sprang up. The eastern part of the townsite saw a hundred saloons, casinos, and dance halls open overnight. Perry seemed determined to outdo its competitors among the frontier boomtowns.

Governor Renfrow appointed a full slate of county officials, with J. C. Scruggs as the first sheriff of County P. Leander Shockey was named the first undersheriff.

U.S. Marshal Nix dispatched Deputy Marshals Bill Tilghman and Heck Thomas to assist in Perry. The marshals worked closely with the sheriff and his men in trying to maintain the peace in the violent frontier town.

The *Perry Independent* described Hell's Half Acre in this routine manner: "Killings averaged a man and a half a day and seemed regarded as merely a minor part of devilment going on among the choicest desperadoes and the scum of half a dozen states."[10]

The sounds of gunfire echoed every night. On September 29, Sheriff Scruggs, his deputies, and the marshals raided the gambling district. The *Oklahoma State Capital* reported: "Wheels of fortune,

faro layouts and chuck-luck tables were piled up outside the princi-
pal resorts in innocuous desuetude . . . The Buckhorn and Blue Bell
[stripped of gaming paraphernalia] looked like deserted tabernacles."[11]

Tilghman and Thomas were appointed city marshals and remained to augment Scruggs' force. Henry S. Johnston, an attorney
who moved to Perry at the opening (and later served as governor of
Oklahoma) made these remarks concerning the sheriff's department:
"While our sheriff was only a 'bull-goose,' he was fortunate in having
three topnotch men on his staff [Taylor, Doyle, and Haines]. They
were obscure but time demonstrated their excellence."[12]

In December of 1893, Congress organized two new judicial districts, each having a U.S. attorney and chief deputy marshal.
Charles Colcord became a chief deputy under Marshal Nix. Haines
received his commission as a U.S. deputy marshal under Colcord
and Nix in 1893.

Haines now had the authority to pursue fugitives into federal
jurisdictions, like the neighboring Osage Indian Reservation. In
thirty years of bringing law and order to the region, he would come
to know the Osage well.

CHAPTER V

OUTLAWS

One of the most notorious and colorful bands of outlaws in the West was the Doolin gang. Bill Doolin was a native of Arkansas who ventured west in 1881. For the next ten years, he worked as a cowboy on ranches in Kansas and Oklahoma. Sometime in 1891, Bill headed down the outlaw trail and joined the infamous Dalton gang.

The Daltons' mother was a Younger, and her nephews were the Youngers who teamed up with Frank and Jesse James to form the most infamous of all outlaw bands, the James-Younger gang. The Daltons introduced Doolin and his cronies Charley Pierce, Bill Power, Dick Broadwell, Little Dick West, and Bitter Creek Newcomb to horse thievery and the art of train robbery.

Doolin, Newcomb, and Pierce split away from the Daltons shortly before their spectacular failed double bank robbery in Coffeyville, Kansas, in 1892. When the smoke cleared, Bill Power, Bob Dalton, Grat Dalton, Dick Broadwell, and four townspeople lay dead.

Meanwhile, Doolin, Newcomb, and Pierce had holed up in Ingalls, near present-day Stillwater, Oklahoma, and formed the core of Bill Doolin's "Wild Bunch." By 1893 Doolin had recruited Tulsa Jack Blake, Dan "Dynamite Dick" Clifton, George "Red Buck" Waightman, and Bill Dalton.

After helping police with the opening of the Cherokee Strip in 1893, newly appointed U.S. Marshal E. D. Nix turned his attention to the Doolin gang. Marshal Nix's office soon learned that the Doolin gang was headquartered in Ingalls.

Doolin and his men were indeed at home in Ingalls, as reported by the *Stillwater Gazette*. Many residents of Ingalls were "in full sympathy with the outlaws, shielding them for the sake of getting their trade.... Whenever an effort is made to capture the gang, they generally have warning and are thus given a chance to escape...."[1]

The gang was regarded by some as local celebrities who were quick to help settlers down on their luck. They were built up by admirers into Robin Hood–like characters. Even U.S. Deputy Marshal Charles Colcord had kind remembrances of Bill Doolin in his autobiography long after his death:

> I was very sorry they had killed old Bill, as he had a great reputation and was not all bad. I had respect for him in many ways, for he was a brave man with many good characteristics. Though he had committed many crimes and carried a high price on his head for robbing the rich, he frequently gave to the poor. A number of people in the Osage country had been helped by receiving from him a cow, a horse, a team, or something they badly needed. Bill was just another one of the men who never could adjust to changing conditions. Charley Vandever, President of the Bank of Pawnee, often talked to me about Bill Doolin and told me that Bill's word was as good as the word of almost any of his customers in the bank.[2]

The banker was particularly impressed when the outlaw took out a $500 loan and repaid it. He also endeared himself to the bank by supposedly preventing it from being robbed on three separate occasions.

U.S. Deputy Marshal Frank Canton also claimed that the help provided to the Doolin gang by the area settlers was due to the personality of Bill Doolin himself. Canton considered Doolin "the squarest and best man" in the gang. "Bill Doolin" said Canton, "had always been kind to the poor settlers, often giving them money to buy groceries." Consequently, "it was almost impossible for a party of officers to travel together through that country without being seen by some friends of the outlaws, who would always give the alarm in time for the criminals to escape."[3]

But the Wild Bunch lived up to the darker side of their reputation on September 1, 1893, in a bloody gun battle with officers at Ingalls.

Three covered wagons containing a score of hidden officers hidden in-
side rolled into Ingalls that quiet morning. The ill-conceived plan to
capture Doolin and his gang turned disastrous for the lawmen, as three
of them were killed, along with two bystanders. Only one gang member was captured, Arkansas Tom Daughtery, and the rest escaped.

The Wild Bunch continued their campaign of robbery, ranging
as far west as Woodward. Guthrie judge Frank Dale ordered
Marshal Nix to instruct his deputies to bring in Doolin's gang dead.
Rewards totaling $5,000 were offered on Bill Doolin's head.

Doolin was finally tracked down and arrested by U.S. Deputy
Marshal Bill Tilghman. Tilghman received a clue that Doolin had
discussed with his physician treatment for his rheumatism at the
mineral baths in Arkansas. Tilghman traced Doolin to Eureka
Springs, where he surprised him in a bathhouse on January 15 and
arrested him. Doolin was returned to Oklahoma and locked up in
the federal jail in Guthrie.

Doolin's incarceration, however, was to be brief. On July 5, he
led an escape from the federal jail that freed thirteen prisoners. One
of the thirteen would cross paths with Wiley Haines years later.
Doolin and Dynamite Dick fled together after stealing a horse and
buggy. U.S. Deputy Marshal Heck Thomas and his men set out in
pursuit of Doolin. Thomas believed that Doolin would return to his
wife and child and centered his search along the Cimarron River
and around Lawson.

U.S. Deputy Marshal Charles Colcord in Perry recruited fellow
officers Wiley Haines and Henry Callahan and rode off in pursuit
as well. They decided to stake out Dynamite Dick's old holdout on
the Big Horseshoe Bend of Hominy Creek. On the trip from Perry,
the marshals made camp, and Callahan shot a covey of quail that
had gone to roost, killing all the birds but one. The men had been
riding hard since daylight and, after roasting the quail, settled in for
a few hours of sleep before daybreak.

They bedded down under a large oak tree that was about four
feet in diameter. The tree stood in the middle of the path they were
traveling on. Callahan and Colcord fell asleep, leaving Haines on
guard. The sleeping men were jolted awake as their horses came
plunging down the path around them. Both men grabbed their
Winchesters and sprang behind a tree, butting each other in the
head so hard they were both knocked to the ground.

Colcord was the first up and saw that the horses were their own. Something had evidently spooked them into the camp while Haines was out on guard. Colcord turned to Callahan, rubbing his head, and said, "Harry, where's your reputation? What do you mean, going to timber like this?"

Callahan looked back at Colcord in his comical Irish way and replied, "Where in the hell's yours?"[4]

None of the escaped prisoners turned up at Dynamite Dick's holdout, so the three lawmen rode the next day to Lawson, in Payne County, where Heck Thomas's posse had headed.

When they arrived, they learned that Thomas's posse had killed Bill Doolin just before their arrival. The body had already been loaded into a spring wagon and started off for Guthrie. Something about the story of Doolin's death evidently bothered Colcord. The posse had stated that they found Doolin walking down a path and he spotted them and raised his rifle to shoot at the officers. The posse filled Bill full of buckshot and Winchester bullets.

Colcord examined the scene of the shooting and was troubled because there was no trace of blood on the ground. Colcord later claimed that Joe Miller, the jailer at Guthrie, found no blood on Doolin's clothes when he undressed the body. Colcord was never satisfied with the posse's story, "although I had some ideas of my own," he concluded. U.S. Deputy Marshal Frank Canton also raised doubts about Heck Thomas's story, but Canton could offer no real proof.

Canton and Thomas never had anything good to say about each other. Canton protested the use of the Dunn brothers by Thomas as posse men and informants. The Dunns had been with Thomas when Doolin was killed, and Canton had proof that the Dunns were murderers and thieves. Canton resented the fact that the Dunns were free to operate in his district under Thomas's protection. Canton even shot and killed Bee Dunn on the streets of Pawnee when the latter confronted him.

Canton took a particular interest in Doolin's demise and felt there was something suspicious about the corpse. "I saw the body myself. It was hot summer weather. Doolin had on a clean, white undershirt, very thin. The shirt had, I think, twenty-three buckshot holes.... Not a particle of dry blood or any other kind on the body and not even a stain of blood on the undershirt. I called the

Doctor's attention to this and I says, 'What does this mean?' He says this means the man was dead before he was shot."[5]

Heck Thomas offered this version of the shooting of Bill Doolin:

> Doolin's wife had told him some of the neighborhood boys had been spying around and that someone was around there that night. Doolin said he would just scare the hell out of them... shoot them up a little if he saw them.... He could have made his escape on the open roads, north, south, east... or through the pasture to the high hills northwest...
>
> Well, he came right down the lane, walking slow in the bright moonlight, Winchester in both hands, well out in front of him... in position to shoot. He was sure on the prowl... I hollered at him... he shot at me and the bullet [missed]. I had let one of the boys have my Winchester and had an old No. 8 shotgun. It was too long in the breech and I couldn't handle it quick so he got another shot with his Winchester... jerked his pistol and some of the boys though he shot once with it. About that time I got the shotgun to work and the fight was over.[6]

Those who claimed Doolin had been shot post-mortem speculated that the outlaw had died from natural causes, with tuberculosis mentioned in some accounts. It is perhaps understandable that some may have believed Bill chronically ill after looking at the post-mortem photographs. Old Bill did not appear to have been enjoying robust health.

Some even claimed that Bill's wife was in on the scheme and took a cut of the reward money. While the Dunn brothers could have easily been involved in such a deception, most doubt that Heck Thomas would have participated.

Wiley Haines never offered an opinion as to how Bill Doolin died. Since he was not a eyewitness, Haines probably did not feel it was his place to draw conclusions. He was not given to speculation and was not a man to speak ill of a fellow officer.

In November of 1897, Dynamite Dick was shot and killed by U.S. Deputy Marshals George Lawson and Hess Bussy. Five months later, the last of Doolin's old gang, Little Dick West, was brought down by Sheriff Frank Rinehart and U.S. Deputy Marshal William Fossett.

The thirteenth man from the famous jailbreak at Guthrie remained at large until 1903, when U.S. Deputy Marshal Wiley Haines captured him in the Osage Nation. Haines was recovering from a near-fatal gunshot wound that he had received in a battle with the Martin brothers. He had just been released from the hospital a few days earlier when he captured outlaw Walter McClain. And so the Daltons and Doolins passed into history.

CHAPTER VI

MORE OUTLAWS

Haines made frequent trips into Indian Territory in pursuit of outlaws. He often traveled through the Osage Nation on official business and came to know the area well. Introducing and selling alcohol to Indians was illegal, and officers fought a constant battle with bootleggers.

Among the worst offenders was the Buchanan gang, which the U.S. Justice Department was eager to put out of business. The Buchanans operated all over northeastern Oklahoma, selling whiskey to the Indians. U.S. Deputy Marshal Colcord took on the job of rounding up the Buchanan gang. Colcord just happened to have an uncle and several friends visiting from Kentucky who were interested in taking a field trip.

Colcord enlisted the help of marshals Frank Canton, Wiley Haines, Ike Steel, and Clarence Young for the expedition. The officers and their guests put together a mess wagon and a complete camp outfit. They set out from Perry and headed east until they reached the old Skiatook trail, which ran through the Osage Nation.

Frank Canton recounted the episode in his autobiography:

> One evening we went into camp rather early on a little creek in the Osage Hills called Boar Creek. While the rest of the party were preparing camp and attending to the stock, Wiley Haines and myself took our fishing tackle and went up the creek a few hundred yards

to see if the fish would bite. It was not long until we had all the fish we wanted. We brought in a string of sixteen black bass, and I do not think that any of them would weight less than three pounds. They were very fat. We baked them in a large Dutch oven and had a royal dinner. Wild turkeys were plentiful and in fine condition. We could kill young turkeys (good frying size) with a shotgun. Our visitors certainly enjoyed themselves.[1]

When the group neared Skiatook at the eastern border of the Osage Reservation, they set up a base camp. A settler named Smith who lived near their camp told the officers that a band of Creeks had gathered at the stomp grounds (Indian dance grounds) on Bird Creek near Skiatook. After supper, five of the marshals, Smith, and one of the visiting Kentuckians set out for the grounds. When they arrived, Canton guessed that 400 men were present, although Colcord puts the figure at 200. The darkness made an estimate difficult.

Colcord described the gathering: "I never saw such a motley crowd in my life and I've seen some bad ones. They were mostly Indians and half breeds, also a lot of hard-looking whites; about 200 men, toughest bunch imaginable."[2]

Canton may not have agreed on their numbers but concurred with Colcord's assessment of the character of the group: "Of all the tough gangs I'd ever seen in my life, the Skiatook dance bunch was the worst."[3]

The deputies moved up and spotted Buchanan serving up whiskey from a barrel in pint cups for twenty-five cents a cup. Canton reported: "a white woman was seated in the hind end of the wagon with a Winchester across her lap, the hammer at full cock, watching every movement. I recognized the man at once. It was Bill Buchanan."[4]

The stomp dance was a couple of miles into Creek country, so the officers were out of their jurisdiction. They lay in wait just across the Osage line, anticipating that the Buchanans would cross into the reservation the next day. The marshals guessed correctly and arrested eighteen men in all according to Colcord. The prisoners were chained together and transported to jail in Guthrie.

Skiatook was also the home of Cattle Annie (Annie McDoulet), who teamed up with Little Breeches (Jennie Stevens) as the teenage sweethearts of the Doolin gang. During the summer of 1895, the pair became well known to officers because they acted as spies for the Doolins.

Jennie Stevens first met Doolin and his gang while sewing up bullet holes in their clothes after a raid, according to Robert DeArment. Jennie joined up with a whiskey peddler and was soon arrested by Frank Canton. Jennie was released on bond and then formed a partnership with Annie McDoulet. Marshal E. D. Nix wrote: "The girls were becoming very troublesome, and it was evident that they were keeping in fairly close touch with the movements of my officers and passing their information along to the outlaws.... Whenever they were seen, they were heavily armed with pistols and Winchesters, and it was reported that they were pretty accurate shots."[5]

Sheriff Lake of Pawnee soon arrested Little Breeches again. The evening of her arrest, a deputy took her to a restaurant for dinner. After eating, she dashed out the back door and escaped on a horse belonging to Frank Canton.

The following day, Canton tracked her to a farmhouse where Little Breeches was holed up with Cattle Annie. The girls fired several shots at the officers before giving up. On August 26, the girls stood trial at Newkirk. Annie was convicted of illegal whiskey sales and sent to reform school in Framingham, Massachusetts. Jennie was convicted of horse theft and sentenced to two years at the Massachusetts Reformatory Prison.

Of all Wiley Haines' fellow officers, none had a more curious background than Frank Canton. Haines worked closely with him on many occasions, pursuing outlaws throughout the territory. When Canton died in 1927, Wiley represented the frontier lawmen associates of Canton at his old friend's funeral.

As Robert K. DeArment writes in his biography of Canton:

Few of the dignitaries attending the funeral knew that the true name of the man they honored was Joe Horner and not Frank Canton, or that his 'picturesque, colorful' history included a criminal career marked by convictions for bank and highway robbery, desperate jail escapes, and indictments for cold-blooded murder... a self-confessed and convicted armed robber and accused back-shooting assassin, he misrepresented himself for fifty years. He had a weakness for alcohol, but he was also a loving family man to whom his wife and daughter were completely devoted. After a wild youth as a vicious desperado, he transformed himself into a frontier lawman and chased felons for almost half a century. He proved to be an intelligent, ambitious, and hardworking peace officer who demonstrated exceptional courage in numerous occasions as he dealt with some of the toughest and most dangerous outlaws in the West.[6]

Canton's father, a Confederate surgeon, died in captivity while Wiley's father, a minister, escaped. Canton's friends "thought he was a remarkably steadfast man and a true comrade, the sort that one could tie to," and "a great character and splendid officer [who] was for law and order as he saw it and did not know the meaning of compromise."

Wiley and Frank had much in common, going all the way back to their childhoods, when both boy's fathers were imprisoned by the Union Army in an Illinois penitentiary.

As a young man, Joe Horner had worked as a cowboy before turning to the outlaw trail from 1874 to 1879. Horner was ultimately sentenced to ten years in prison at Huntsville, Texas, for robbery. On August 4, 1879, Horner escaped from prison, took the name Frank Canton, and fled to Wyoming.

Initially he worked as a cowboy, then became an inspector for the Wyoming Stock Raisers' Association, and was elected sheriff of Johnson County in 1882. He was appointed U.S. deputy marshal in 1885 and served a second two-year term as sheriff. Canton then took a job as a detective in Wyoming before moving on to Oklahoma Territory to serve as under sheriff of the new County Q (Pawnee County) in 1894.

Canton managed to hide his outlaw days, fabricating a past to fill the gaps. There is no evidence that any of Canton's fellow officers, with the exception of his brother and his old friend and cowboy partner Sheriff Frank Lake, were aware of his criminal past. Canton's experience on both sides of the law seemed to enhance his effectiveness as an officer.

Frank was particularly disturbed with U.S. Deputy Marshal Heck Thomas's practice of using known criminals like the Dunn brothers as members of his posses. The Dunns were known to Canton as cattle thieves and murderers and enjoyed the protection of Heck Thomas and Bill Tilghman because of their cooperation with them. Thomas and Tilghman would be joined by Marshal Chris Madsen to be immortalized as "The Three Guardsmen." While Colcord and Canton raised serious questions in regard to Tilghman and Thomas's methods and results, Chris Madsen was apparently held in universal respect.

Madsen served as chief U.S. deputy marshal for many years and served as U.S. marshal of Oklahoma for a brief time. Although Madsen had a distinguished career as a lawman, his years of professional soldiering were even more fascinating.

Madsen was a Dane who immigrated to the United States in 1876 and enlisted in the U.S. Army. He had come to fight Indians. Homer Croy's book *Trigger Marshal* summarizes Madsen's military career before coming to the states:

> Chris told how he had fought in the Danish Army, when he was fourteen, against the Germans, and how the Danes had lost. Then how he had joined the French Foreign Legion and been assigned to the Chasserus d'Afrique and sent to Algeria. He had been serving with his unit, in the province of Oran, when the Franco-Prussian War broke out, and he had returned with his outfit and fought the Germans at the Battle of Sedan. Things had gone a little wrong; he had been wounded, captured, and put in prison. But not for long. He had escaped and returned to France where he has fought with the guerrillas and other irregulars. Then out of the clear blue sky the war was over and Chris had been sent back to Algeria where he had completed his five-year enlistment in the French Foreign Legion.[7]

When researchers finally began digging into Madsen's past, a lot of inconsistencies turned up. In 1995 Leif Ernst uncovered the truth.[8] Ernst discovered that Madsen had falsified his place of birth in Denmark, making it very difficult for his past to be traced. Ernst found that Madsen had never served in the Danish army or the French Foreign Legion. But he did serve five different sentences in the Copenhagen prison for convictions of fraud, forgery, begging, and vagrancy.

It also appears that the Danish government deported Madsen to the United States, where he promptly enlisted in the army. While in the army, he served a five-month sentence in the Wyoming Territorial Prison for larceny. In later years, Madsen embellished his imaginary exploits, subscribing to the philosophy that writer Nancy Samuelson aptly described as, "If you can't improve on the story there's no point in telling it."[9] As an officer, Madsen spent little time actually in the field pursuing outlaws. He primarily functioned as an office deputy.

There were many other U.S. deputy marshals with equally impressive records who didn't get the press that Tilghman in particular sought out. Colcord, Canton, Haines, Ledbetter, Callahan, and others could have easily been added to the triumvirate of Tilghman, Thomas, and Madsen.

Wiley Haines even expressed distaste privately about Bill Tilghman's road show, "The Passing of the Outlaws." Tilghman in later years had a movie made featuring his exploits as a lawman and toured the country, charging admission. To make matters worse, the movie had numerous factual errors, such as giving Tilghman credit for taking out the Martin gang, which was actually accomplished by Wiley Haines and Warren Bennett.

To Haines and many of the other old-time officers, calling attention to one's professional accomplishments seemed to lack dignity. Most of the real officers had placed their lives in jeopardy many times, and some had paid the ultimate price. A road show seemed to demean what these courageous men had stood for.

If Haines ever suspected Frank Canton's outlaw past, he never gave any indication. Even if Haines had known, it was not likely to have affected their friendship. He judged a man by who he was, not what he might have been. Nor did Haines hold a grudge; the first man he escorted off the Osage Reservation later became a close personal friend. His presence as an honorary pallbearer at Canton's funeral demonstrated the high regard he held for his comrade.

CHAPTER VII

THE OSAGE NATION

After serving several terms as undersheriff in Perry, Haines moved his family to a ranch near Clifton, a small community about fifteen miles from Shawnee. While at Clifton, he sat for the Civil Service exam and passed it. He received an appointment from the Department of Interior as a constable for the Indian police in the Osage Nation.

Although Haines' headquarters were to be in Pawhuska, the capital of the Osage, he located his family in Hominy, a small community about twenty miles south of Pawhuska. The family packed their household goods and farming tools into four big wagons and set out on the two-week journey from Clifton to Hominy. The roads were bad, and numerous streams had to be forded by the teams and wagons.

In addition, Haines had acquired 100 head of good "white-lined" cattle, and these were driven by six or seven cowboys. The move was a great adventure for the three children, John, Mary, and Wiley Jr., as the family camped out each night and cooked their meals over the fire.

The final hurdle in the journey was crossing the Arkansas River near Cleveland to enter the Osage. It was on the banks of the Arkansas that the family made the first of many friends in the new country. The Stout family lived on the river, near a cable-operated ferry. In an interview on her eighty-first birthday, Sarah Haines told the story of the first woman to extend a friendly hand to her, Mrs. A.H. Stout: "Mrs. Stout came out with a pan heaped with hot biscuits and a big pot of hot coffee. Those were beyond a doubt the best biscuits I ever ate and the best coffee I ever tasted."[1] The gesture began a friendship between the two families that lasted for generations.

The four laden wagons were ferried across the river, and the cattle were swum across. But the family's luck was about to run out.

"The cattle didn't much more than hit the Osage until we lost nearly every one of them from Texas fever," Sarah recounted.[2] The bovine illness was an especially virulent form of pneumonia that was highly contagious.

Hominy was little more than a post with a general store, a blacksmith shop, and a few houses in the summer of 1898. The only place available for the family to stay in town was an empty store building. They then lived for a time on Nicacola Creek, or Haines Creek, as it became known, where their fourth child, Rhalls, was born. They later leased land south of Black Dog Camp, where Haines broke the virgin land and farmed in his spare time.

Ten years after they arrived in the Osage, Haines bought a town lot and erected an eight-room house, which was nearly encircled by a porch. He hauled gravel from a creek and built the first residential concrete sidewalk in town. A log barn was also built (it stood where the old First National Bank building was located). Sarah recalled that there was so much spring rain that the logs of the new barn sprouted leaves. The pasture fence ran along what is now the main street of Hominy.

When the townsite was later laid out, the entire house was jacked up and moved by mules to its present location, at 327 Haines Avenue. As the family grew, more rooms were added, doubling the size of the house. As Haines settled into his duties, Sarah managed the household from which Wiley was frequently absent. Sarah spent many worried days never knowing if her children's father would be slain by a bandit's bullet.

Haines acquired a reputation as an effective and honest lawman. The *Osage Journal* of May 16, 1901, remarked: "Wiley Haines, one of our able constables, was in town Friday and Saturday from his Hominy district. We will bet a coon skin there is not a district throughout the reservation that is better presided over than the one

Wiley has. Wiley is a man that believes in all things good and condemns wrong. Wiley has many staunch friends on the reservation."[3]

Haines also had some dangerous enemies. He was wounded in three separate gun battles and shot at from ambush on several occasions. Even Sarah was once shot at by an unknown sniper. One day while Haines was away in Pawhuska, Sarah was at home tending to chores. She stepped out on the back porch to empty a pan of dishwater. When she threw the water from the pan, a shot rang out from Haines Hill above the house, slapping the pan from her hands. The area was searched, but the shooter was never found.

Sarah's life on the frontier was a challenge. "All merchandise was freighted in," she recalled. "That was before there was a railroad here. Groceries were brought by freighter from Elgin, Kansas. A mail hack carried the mail back and forth to Elgin and we were lucky to get mail once a week.

"There were no church buildings and no school buildings here when we first came to town and only a few houses. There was a blacksmith shop... a hotel and barber shop... a general merchandise store... and a bakery... Everything was done by horse or mule power... I remember the excitement when the first passenger train ran through Hominy. It was in 1904 and was a special to the World's Fair in St. Louis, Missouri."[4]

Sarah saw that her nine children (John, Mary, Wiley Jr., Rhalls, Elma, Robert, Virgil, Warren, Ironica) all attended school and Sunday school. She raised them with the values to grow into good citizens. She also taught them that busy hands and hard work would keep them out of mischief.

Reverend and Mrs. John W. Haines, parents of Wiley G. Haines. Reverend Haines was one of the founders of Southwest Baptist College, Bolivar, Missouri.

Wiley Green Haines
Age approx. mid-twenties, taken in 1880s, possibly in San Francisco.

Wiley Haines as a young man.

Marriage picture. Wiley G. Haines and Sarah E. Tapp, Oklahoma City, O.T., 1892.

Wiley G. Haines and wife Sarah.

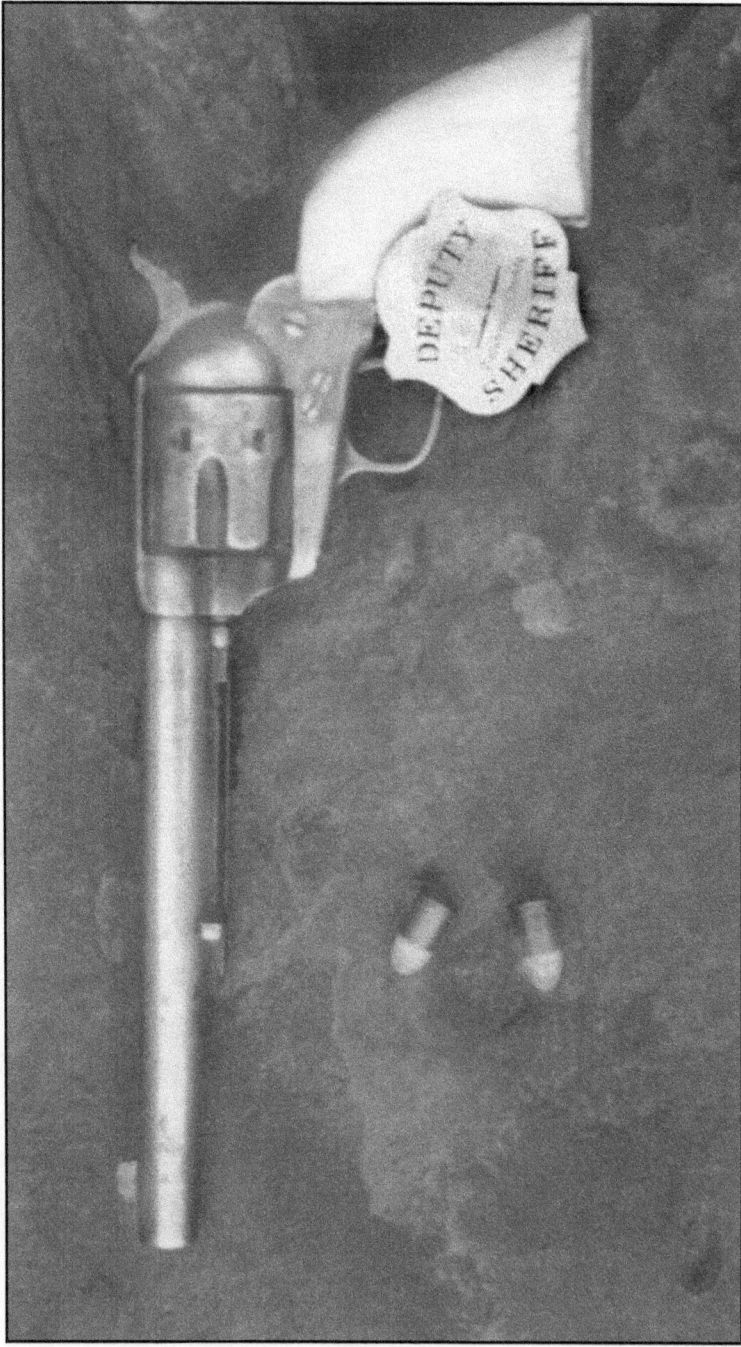

Colt .44 given to Marshal Haines in 1890 with inscription on back strap—"Wiley G. Haines from C. H. Deford" Captian Deford was the first sheriff of Oklahoma City. Deputy sheriff badge with inscription; W. G. Haines; Oklahoma County.

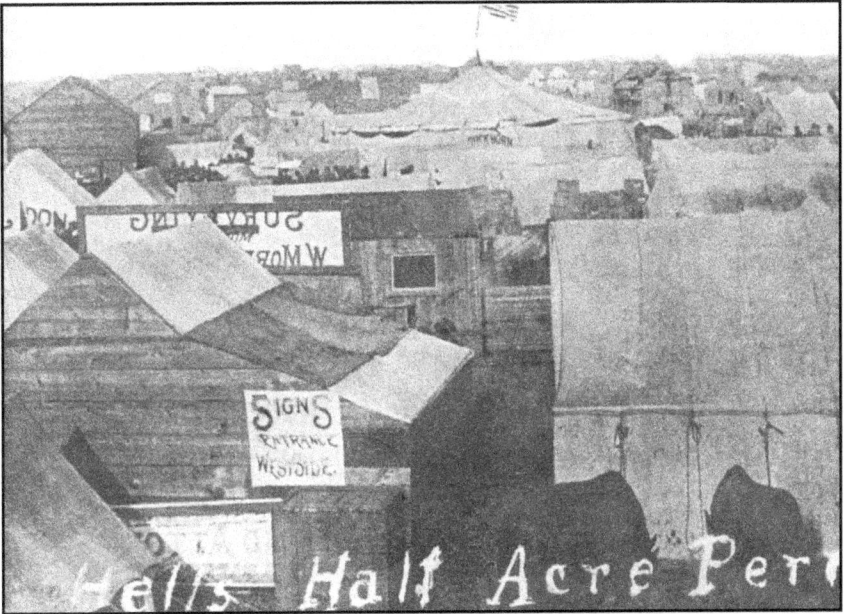

Hell's Half Acre, Perry, Oklahoma, 1893.

Pawhaska, capital of the Osage Reservation, 1890s.

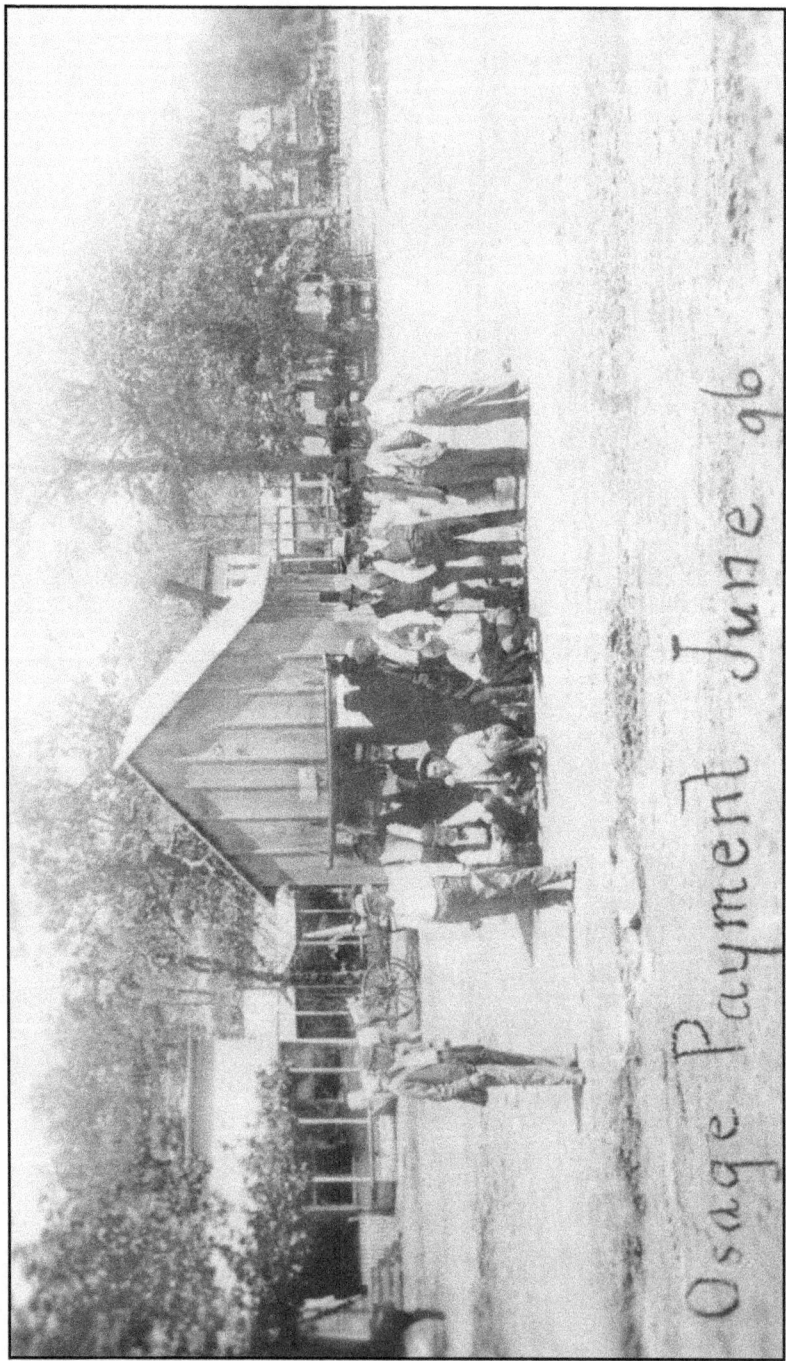

Osage Payment June 96

Marshal Wiley Haines, third from right, standing; Marshal Warren Bennett, second from right, standing. June 1896, Pawhuska.

Wiley Haines on horseback.

Taken at Pawhuska, Oklahoma, in 1900.

Marshal Haines on horse at approximately the site where the triangle building is presently located.

Osage Indian Round House Indian Village, Hominy, Oklahoma. Early 1900s.

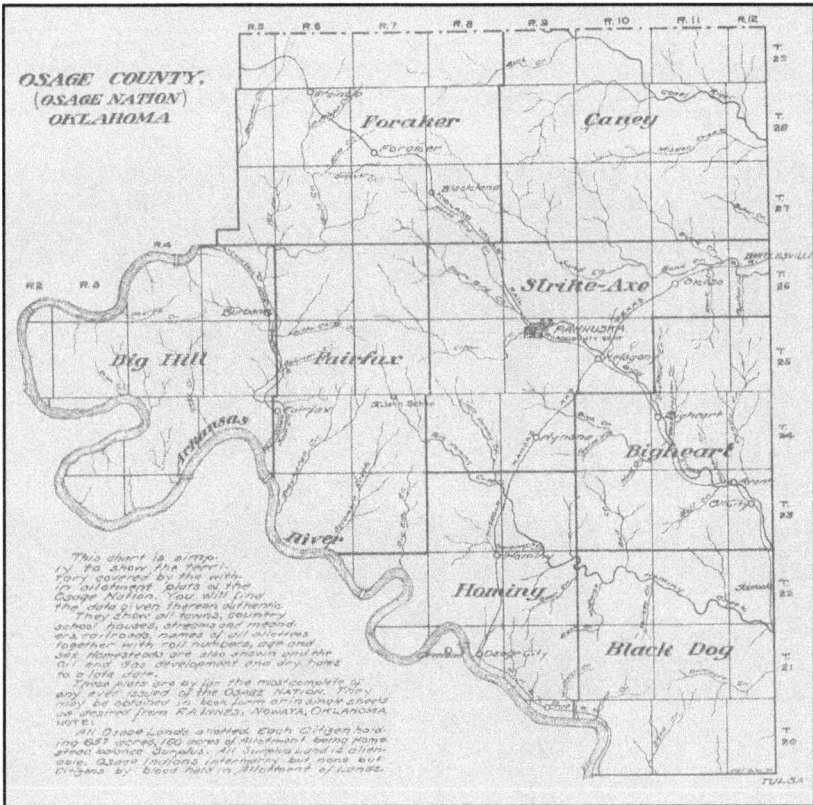

U.S. Deputy Marshal Warren Bennett.

Wiley G. Haines, third from right, with badge and pistol,
at Osage Indian payment in Pawhuska.

Parade, Main Street of Hominy, I.T.

Wiley Haines family portrait, 1900.

View of Hominy from "Haines Hill."
Wiley Haines home is large white house in right foreground.

Wiley G. Haines home in Hominy.

Deputy Marshal Bill Tilghman

Chris Madsen, one of Custer's scouts in the 7th Cavalry, was left for dead on battle-field at Wounded Knee. Later became Deputy U.S. Marshal out of Fort Smith, Wichita, and Guthrie courts.

Deputy Marshal Heck Thomas.
Photo from the Heck Thomas Collection, courtesy Beth Thomas Meeks.

Bill Tilghman and C. F. Colord, Deputy U.S. Marshals, at the opening of Cherokee Strip, Perry, Oklahoma, September 1893.

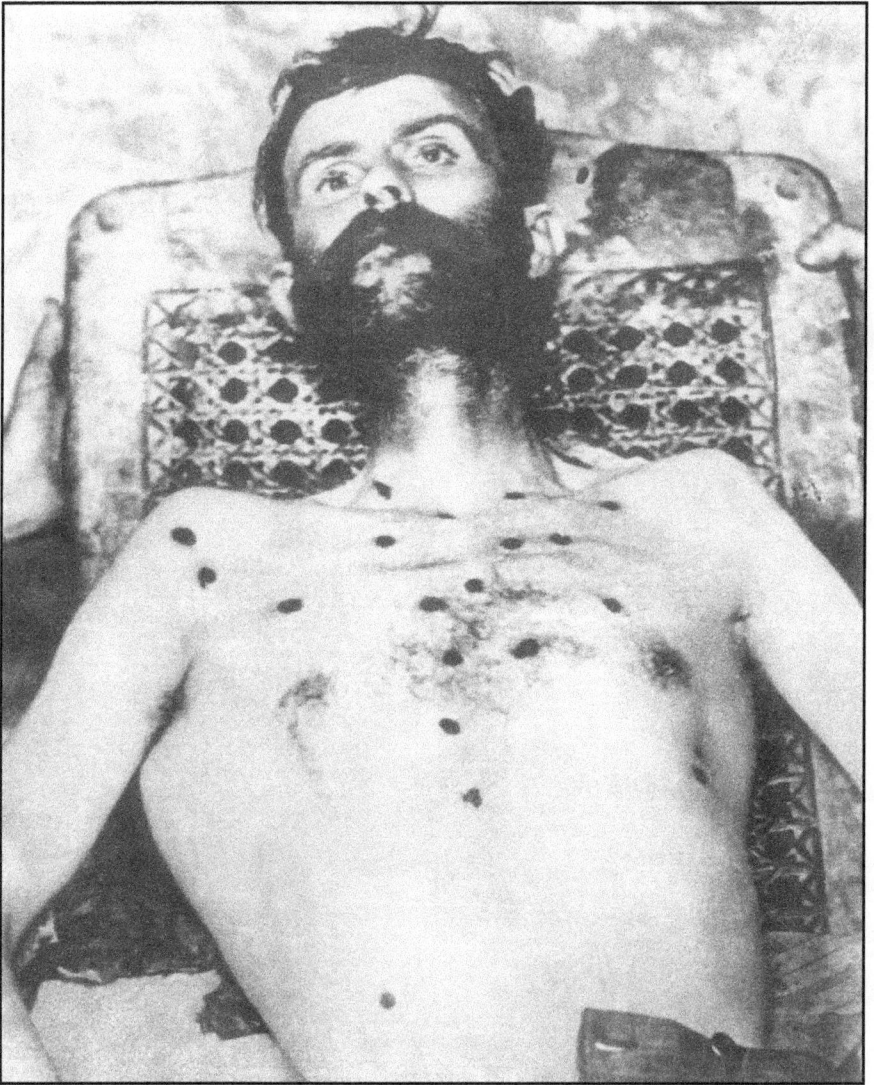

Bill Doolin, leader of the famous Doolin outlaw gang, Oklahoma.

Wooster Mound.

Sam and Will Martin, in death, and horses, saddles, ammo, rifles, revolvers, taken when they were caught. August 8, 1903, near Wooster Mound, Osage Reservation.

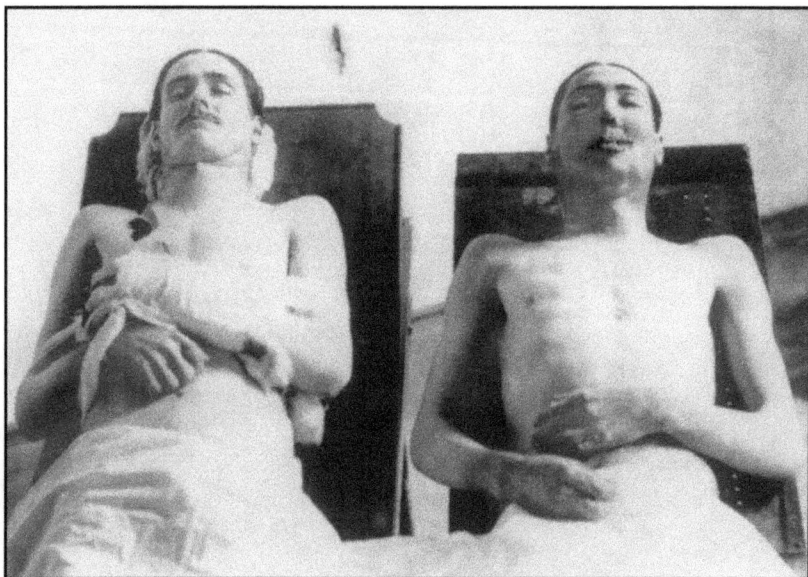

Sam and Will Martin, in death. August 9, 1903.

TWO GOOD
DESPERADOES

———

Occupy Slabs at the Guthrie
Morgue.

———

THE MARTIN BROTHERS

Top: Sam Martin
(left) and Will Martin
(right) on slabs in
undertaking parlor
at Guthrie, Okla-
homa Territory. Left:
*Oklahoma State
Capital*, August 12,
1903.

view of W. DeWitte's abhorrence of trusts, the correspondent adds, it is doubtful whether he will accept the bait.

TWO OUTLAWS ARE DEAD.

Effective Work by a Posse Near Pawhuska, Ok.—Long List of Crimes Perpetrated by the Gang.

Guthrie, Ok., Aug. 11.—The two members of the Martin gang of outlaws, who engaged in a fight Saturday with a posse of deputy sheriffs in the Osage Indian nation, are dead. Deputy Marshal Haines, who was shot, is improving. The other members of the gang escaped but are still being pursued. Two months ago they held up and robbed nearly 100 travelers on a lonely road. They also are charged with killing a citizen in the robbery of the railway station at Hennessey, Ok., with killing City Marshal Cross. of Geary, and with robbing the post office at Hopeton.

LEFT HER BUSTLE AT HOME.

Kansas Woman Who Thought She Had Lost $7,300 Started Something While Traveling in Minnesota.

St. Paul, Minn., Aug. 11.—Word was received by union depot officials that the missing bustle, in which $7,300 had been sewed by Mrs. Lucy Van Cerke, of Shawnee, Kan., and which she supposed she had dropped from a train while en route to St. Paul, has been found. Mrs. Van Cerke in the hurry of leaving her old home had forgotten

...strike water. They are still selling town lots in Hominy, O. T.

Deputy United States Marshal Wiley Haines brought in two prisoners charged with stealing five head of horses from Che-sho-hun-kah near Grayhorse, on last Saturday night. Mr. Hanes trailed these men for about two hundred miles. At Tulsa he was joined by Deputy United States Marshal H. A. Thomson of the Western District of I. T. and when overtaken in the Greenleaf mountains of the Cherokee country, they were still in possession of the horses stolen. The horses were returned to the owner Che-sho-hun-kah. The prisoners gave the names of C. W. Bailey and J. T. Thompson. They were arraigned before United States Commissioner E. N. Yates, and plead not guilty. Their bond was fixed at $1,000 each, and in default of same were remanded to jail at Guthrie.

CHAPTER VIII

PEACEMAKER OF THE OSAGE

When Haines reported for duty to the federal Indian agent, Colonel J. W. Pollock, in Pawhuska, he found that Pollock had a problem with his credentials. Pollock resented the fact that Haines had obtained his appointment through the Civil Service. He incorrectly assumed that Haines was unfamiliar with the Osage and would be ill-prepared to deal with the demanding duties of the reservation.

As a test, Pollock immediately ordered Haines to escort a tough character named Henry Behining off the reservation. Whites living and working on the reservation were required to pay one dollar a month, and Behining had refused to pay his fee. He had a reputation as a man who wouldn't back down. Pollock privately doubted that Haines could accomplish his assignment.

Haines calmly rode out to face Behining and informed him of his purpose. Behining showed the expected initial resistance, but Haines stood his ground. Behining must have seen the determination in Haines' steel-gray eyes as he faced him down. Haines escorted his man to Pawhuska and off the reservation.

Not unexpectedly, Haines and Henry Behining later wound up on friendly terms. As Haines recalled, "Henry returned later to become Osage County's first engineer. We were always the best of friends."[1]

Colonel Pollock was pleasantly surprised at how Haines had taken a potentially lethal situation and resolved it in a nonviolent and professional manner. Haines was promoted to assistant chief of the Osage Indian Police under Chief Warren Bennett. Like Haines, Bennett also carried a commission as a U.S. deputy marshal. The pair became a relentless team in enforcing the law on the wild 1.5 million-acre reservation.

At the time of Haines' arrival in the Osage Nation in 1898, he had this to say about the general conditions: the country was "teeming with whiskey peddlers and horse thieves. What few were not following this living were cowed by the lawless and many failed to cooperate with the officers. This made it hard for the officers to discharge their duties."[2]

The Osage tribe had roamed the plains hunting buffalo and fighting their ancestral enemies until they were relocated by the federal government in 1872. The 1.5 million-acre reservation was purchased from Cherokee lands for the tribe and was overseen by Indian agents from the U.S. Department of Interior.

Haines acquired an intimate knowledge of the proud Osage people and worked tirelessly on their behalf. White men continually encroached upon the reservation, coveting the lush bluestem pastures and preying upon Indian livestock. When Haines arrived, he joined Warren Bennett and a handful of constables in patrolling the vast reservation. Haines became fluent in the Osage language, which accorded him a special status within the tribe.

He counted many of the great chiefs of the Osage among his friends, such as Black Dog, Bacon Rind, and Fred Lookout. The Osage expressed their appreciation to Haines by presenting him with fine gifts, including a gold French pocket watch and an engraved revolver with a pearl handle.

When vast reserves of oil were later discovered in the Osage, Haines watched the 2,229-member tribe become fabulously wealthy. Haines' duties included guarding the enormous royalty payments made quarterly to the tribe.

One of the more curious episodes in Haines' career nearly sent him on a mission halfway around the world. After defeating Spain in 1898, the U.S. was wrestling with its first colonial problems in the newly acquired Philippines. Colonel Pollock was so impressed with Haines' performance that he formally offered his services to the U.S. War Department for the capture of the Philippino rebel Emilio Aguinaldo.

Aguinaldo, who had supported the Americans in the war against Spain, now turned against his new master, America. Aguinaldo and his rebel army fought guerrilla-style from the Philippine jungles. Pollock maintained that Haines, with his experience in pursuing and capturing outlaws in the Osage wilderness, could locate and subdue Aguinaldo in a matter of weeks.

The War Department declined Pollock's offer and instead gave the job to Major Frederick Funston and the 20th Kansas Infantry. Eighteen months later, Aguinaldo was finally captured.

Pursuing outlaws was not the only duty that occupied a deputy marshal's time. One chore, taking the census, helped acquaint Haines with all the tribal members. A daily routine was checking the permits of whites to determine if they were legal residents of the reservation.

Since the Osage was largely rural, farming and ranching were the mainstays of the economy until oil was discovered. Many of the crimes involved stolen livestock. Not only did Haines and other officers have the responsibility of arresting the thieves, but they also had to return or otherwise dispose of recovered animals or strays. When the owners could not be located, stray notices were published in the local papers. The January 3, 1901, issue of the *Osage Journal* contained the following stray notices:

> The following property will be sold to the highest bidder at public auction for cash in hand on Monday, January 7, 1901, unless proved within sixty days.
>
> 1—Iron gray pony, 4 years old, no brand or mark. Posted by Wiley G. Haines, constable.
> 2—One yellow pony, 2 years old, no brand or mark. Posted by Wiley G. Haines, constable.
> 3—One yellow cow about 16 years old, weight about 600 pounds, big knot on right side, branded 'HR' on right hip. Posted by Wiley G. Haines, constable.
> 4—One roan cow about 14 years old, weight about 750 pounds, branded 'TR' on right hip. Posted by Wiley G. Haines, constable.[3]

Annual reports submitted by the Indian Agent made numerous references to the illegal liquor traffic. The battle against bootleggers for "introducing" liquor was never-ending. One agent noted with pride that no saloons operated within the Osage Reservation. But he did concede that "Osage Indians, both men and women, have formed the habit of going to border towns for the express purpose of getting drunk and procuring a supply of liquor. The towns most frequented for this purpose are Cushing, Pawnee, Ponca City, Bartesville and Tulsa. Some go as far as Joplin, Kansas City and other towns located at a distance to procure liquor."[4]

It was also noted that the Osages did not brew any intoxicating liquors. As the suppression of the liquor traffic became more effective, whiskey, beer, and wine became scarce. Alcoholics were forced to find substitutes, like one called "Jake," composed of ginger and alcohol. Lemon extracts, patent medicines, and even hair tonic were turned to in desperation. Occasionally, methanol was inadvertently consumed, resulting in numerous deaths. The May 4, 1905, issue of the *Pawhuska Journal Capital* described this episode:

> The city was startled Monday morning to learn of the sudden death of Wesley Carrington, who lived in Pawhuska one block east of the Baptist Church. At the same time, it was learned that four laborers in the railroad camp near the graveyard in the northwest of town were sick and in the afternoon two of them died. On Tuesday morning another one died and in the afternoon the fifth one passed away. Investigation disclosed the fact that they had been drinking bay rum [hair tonic] made with wood alcohol instead of grain alcohol.[5]

In contrast, the agents generally had a very liberal view of the use of peyote. By 1916 one agent noted that

> the use of peyote or mescal is indulged to a considerable extent in religious services. There are not less than 20 mescal churches scattered about the reservation, and the services are conducted at these places weekly. A great many of the Osages have been converted and I have not noticed any evil effect either physically or mentally from the use of the drug. It is true that those who have made a careful investigation of the effects of this drug claim it injurious. The mescal Indians are temperate and are bitterly opposed to the use of alcoholic liquor.[6]

Gambling, however was considered an "evil," and that the agents tried in vain to control it:

Like all other Indians, the Osages are inveterate gamblers, and play cards and Indian dice games to some extent. The practice of gambling among the Osage is of long standing and is indulged in as often as condition will permit ... The stakes played for are not large as a rule, and the practice is one of pastime and does not have as its subject material gain. Indians have been cautioned to desist from gambling, but there is no doubt that they play when not observed. Several Indians were arrested for gambling during the past year, but I understand that the case was dismissed.[7]

Osage stomp dances were tolerated as well.

The Osages frequently have stomp dances, but I do not believe that their indulgences in this pastime has had the effect on demoralizing their morals or retarding their advancement ... the majority of Indians are elder Indians. On account of the harmless character of the Osage stomp dance, I am inclined to be lenient and allow them to continue this form of pastime when not indulged in too frequently.[8]

For nearly a year, Haines kept a daily logbook detailing his many encounters. The entries span the months at the turn of the century, from 1899 to 1900. It is a pity that only such a brief record survives, but it nonetheless gives a good insight into the day-to-day life of a frontier marshal. Some of the entries are as follows:

May 24, 1899 Went to see Black Dog to try and get him to influence Osages to follow and catch horse and cow thieves that made raids on them while I was away. Also asked him to influence his followers to answer questions when I was trying to get statistics. He agreed to do both.

June 7, 1899 I called on Mose Cedars and found a little negro boy working for him, about 15 years old. I directed him to notify Matt and Joe Gasgin to get off the Osage Reservation as they are horse thieves and bad characters. Also tried to prevail on him to quit making his house a den of thieves.

June 15, 1899 Went to Pawhuska as per order of Agent to assist in the preservation of good order during payment.

June 23, 1899 Saw S.W. Brown who claims to be a squaw man and didn't need any permit. After he left I found he was lying. I overtook him and started him out of the Osage Reservation.

June 26, 1899 Went to Hominy Post, interviewed many parties

that I had notified about their permits as can be seen by referring to preceding pages. [Wiley's journal is full of hundreds of entries concerning checking permits for residing and working in the Osage. It appears that many did not have valid permits. Part of Wiley's daily duty involved checking permits and escorting offenders off the reservation.]

June 30, 1899 Went south of Hominy Post to see about stock reported to be held by thief (Alex Ingram) in John Logan's pasture. Found. It was a mistake.

July 3, 1899 Worked on statistics.

July 4, 1899 Tried to locate thieves that stole harnesses this morning. Went to bar-be-que at Martin's on Birch Creek, 8 miles north of Pawhuska. Everything quiet and peaceable.

July 13, 1899 Went with Captain Ransom Payne to Black Dog Camp and found several Caddo and Delaware Indians visiting.

July 19, 1899 I arrested J. Labdell for trespassing on Osage Reservation. Took him home, kept him overnight. On July 20, took him across the river to Cleveland and directed him to stay off the Osage Reservation.

July 22, 1899 F.W. Wilson [who had been working for Black Dog] was turned over to me by Deputy Sheriff J.N. Hewitt. Hewitt claiming that Wilson had stolen a horse from him and rode it to death.

July 24, 1899 Sent James Binkford to Pawhuska with F.W. Wilson. He returned in the afternoon with Wilson, the U.S. Commissioner having fixed his bond at 500 dollars. Got 310 pounds of ice.

July 27, 1899 Stayed at home most of the day. Went to Hominy Post in the afternoon. At 9 P.M. my wife was confined, giving birth to a fine baby boy. Dr. Morphis attending.

August 1, 1899 Started to Hominy Post and met Alex Ingram whom I tried to capture but he being on horseback and I in a buggy, he got away.

August 14, 1899 Meet Bud Trail, a U.S. Deputy Marshal at Claremore, I.T. Go with him east to Laughlin's. Meet U.S. Deputy Marshal Warren Bennett. We go to Glenn Flippens and arrest him for murdering one J. Williams.

August 15, 1899 Go to Tulsa, I.T. Arrest Jack Harlow, who is accused of being one of the murderers of Williams. Also arrest Obermeyer for burning out Stonebraker's brand on one of Stonebraker's strays. Stay all night at Jack Whalin's.

August 18, 1899 Return home—got to hominy and receive anonymous letter signed, 'House Crik' threatening to kill me if I don't leave the country before court.

August 31, 1899 Go to Hominy Post then south several miles. Arrest Dan Kendrick and Arthur Wainscott for being drunk.

September 5, 1899 Agent Pollock sends me out to try and find Z.T. Alred who is accused of raping an eight year old girl. I go to Bigheart's. Find that Alred has several hours start on me. I follow him by tracks until he quits the trail. I go to new railroad and look for him. Send word everywhere I can. Search several railroad camps and Skullot's house about 11 P.M.

September 6, 1899 Still hunt for Alred on down railroad grade, below Austin P.O. then go back to agency via Collon's ranch.

September 11, 1899 Take Russell Warrior to Elgin, Kansas, so that he may go to school.

September 18, 1899 Monday night Constable John Plummer and I take thirteen Indian boys to Elgin, Kansas for Dr. Divan, who is aiming to take them to Carlisle, Pennsylvania.

September 19. 1899 Arrest Wm. Linn about 12:30 A.M. for introducing beer and whiskey.

September 23, 1899 Arrest Jack Harlow for stealing cattle.

September 24, 1899 Went to Alex Davis' and hunted for George Denver who is accused of larceny of hogs from John McCoy.

September 25, 1899 Went to Denver's and got him. Went north through Skiatook. Searched along the line for Glenn Flippens, who is wanted for almost every crime.

September 26, 1899 Went to Henry Behining's on Birch Creek. Bennett arrested him and Alsie Gunn. Charged with introducing liquor.

October 5, 1899 Went to Hominy and then in hills looking for intruders.

October 21, 1899 Go north 5 or 6 miles. Also go over to Olo-hap-mal-ah farm and try to settle dispute between him and James Hall. Settled?

October 21, 1899 Hear of outlaw in vicinity by name of Frank Watkins. Up all night. Catch him at daylight Sunday morning, Oct. 22/99.

October 23, 1899 Go with Watkins to Pawhuska. Turn him over to Warren Bennett. Receive orders to go to Mrs. Maggie Lawrence's 10 miles southeast of Arkansas City and settle dispute between Maggie Lawrence and tenant, Mr. Avant.

October 24, 1899 Go to Kaw Agency with Special Agent G.B. Pray.

October 25, 1899 Go to Lawrence farm. Find the matter practically settled, return to Kaw Agency.

October 26, 1899 Go to Grayhorse. It rains.

November 8, 1899 Go to Pawnee to attend court.

November 10, 1899 At Pawnee arrest John McPherson in the act of giving an Osage Indian some whiskey.

November 25, 1899 Am discharged as witness at Pawnee at 5 P.M.

December 4, 1899 Go to Pawhuska to attend payment.

December 11–15, 1899 Worked around agency doing police duty.

December 17, 1899 Track horse thieves all day.

December 18, 1899 Notify Eugene Ware who is taking mescal how he can recover his horse that was stolen Saturday night. He refused to make any effort to recover the horse. Said, "Let it go."

December 25, 1899 I go to banquet and ball at Jap Riddles', watched all night but failed to catch any whiskey or peddlers.

December 29, 1899 I try to locate or find some whiskey, also look out for intruders or hunters. Ride nearly all day.

January 1, 1900 New Years' Day finds me riding in the snow.

January 6, 1900 Worked out northwest of Hominy looking for intruders and hunters. Also rounded up a lot of Indian children for school.

January 8, 1900 Arrest Steve Ballew in night for drunkenness.

January 10, 1900 Receive orders to capture three Indian boys that ran away from government schools. Go southwest of Pawhuska. Ride about twenty-five miles and return to Pawhuska without finding them. Go to Hominy that night.

January 11, 1900 Find boys in brush, running northwest of Hominy about six miles. Take them back to school.

January 12, 1900 Work around agency. Go southeast twenty miles looking for intruders. Also try to capture outlaws (with Deputy Marshal Bennett). Return to Pawhuska.

January 15, 1900 Went north in search of Arthur Wainscott who is wanted for stealing hogs.

January 29, 1900 Receive letter from acting agent W.D. Leonard directing that I quarantine against other parts of Oklahoma and Kansas (due to smallpox outbreak).

January 30, 1900 Put in time quite busily in trying to establish quarantine around Hominy.

January 31, 1900 Posting up notices and turning people back.

February 4, 1900 Am notified that horse thieves have again made raid on Indian horses. Perry King tells me they are on trail north of Hominy Post.

I go north of Hominy post about one-half mile and strike the trail. Ho-ke-os-ah and Perry King follow the trail, being joined by Tom Gilliland. With some difficulty we follow the trail near J.L. Freeman's. He joins us. We follow about 8 miles east of there and discover the parties have quit the trail. But two of them have come back, evidently on lookout. We find the trail again and soon discover the horses.

After having ridden the trail 35 miles we advance afoot. I send Perry King across branch. Tell Freeman to watch to the left and Tom Gilliland to go to my right. We advance. I observe several objects through the brush of the blackjack trees. I call, "Hey there! Hold up your hands!" I see a commotion but no sign of obeyance to the order. I fire and advance two or three steps. Call again, "Hold up your hands!" Am not obeyed. I fire again and advance and see two persons with hands up. I discover that what I think is a third person is a saddle. I find that I have fatally shot two horse thieves, one named Arthur Brooksher and the other gave his name as Henry Myers. I send for doctor. He advises that we remove Myers to a house. We go to house, but when we arrive Myers is dead. Brooksher having died very soon after being shot. I go with corpses to J.L. Freeman's place. Stay all night, next day.

February 5, 1900 Take bodies of parties killed yesterday to agency. Acting Agent Wm. Leonard had them taken charge of by undertakers. They had five head of Indian horses with them.

February 6, 1900 Myself and other witnesses are examined by a coroner's jury and I was exonerated from all blame and it was a justifiable act of self-defense.

February 8, 1900 Appoint J.L. Freeman quarantine guard at Tulsa. Return to Hominy.

February 10, 1900 Go to Pawhuska to see agent and get Dr. Morphis to examine parties at C. McKenzies and L.J. Riddles to see if they have small pox.

February 11, 1900 Return to Hominy with Deputy U.S. Marshal Warren Bennett. Appoint D.H. Harris quarantine guard at C. McKenzies and H.R. Adams at L.J. Riddles.

February 12, 1900 Bennett and I go east looking for outlaws. Stay all night at Lou Appleby's.

February 13, 1900 We find James Cordell, who has tried to give us the dodge. Bennett takes him to Pawhuska and I go to Hominy.

February 14–15, 1900 Busy as quarantine guard.

February 19, 1900 Go to Pawhuska to see about raising quarantine at L.J. Riddles. Agent says it's best to wait a while.

February 20, 1900 Return to Hominy.[9]

CHAPTER IX

THE RISE OF THE MARTIN GANG

Of the innumerable confrontations with lawbreakers of every description during Haines' long career, none were more notorious or dangerous than the Martin brothers. Western historians have mostly neglected the exploits of the Martins. While the Dalton, Doolin, James, and other gangs occupied the spotlight, the Martins surpassed them all.

At the nucleus of the Martin gang were brothers Samuel and William Martin, whom author Glenn Shirley describes as "hell-raising farm boys." The description accurately depicts their early years. The brothers were the sons of Luther Martin, who had moved the family from Kansas to Oklahoma Territory in 1889.

As the boys grew up, they fell into increasingly serious trouble in the nearby town of Mulhall. One day they shot up the town, causing a wagon and team of horses to run away, almost wrecking the wagon. The wagon belonged to Charles Hull, who filed charges against the Martin brothers. Luther Martin approached Hull about dropping the charges in exchange for a financial settlement, but Hull refused.

Soon after, on May 22, 1889, Hull, his wife and their seven-year-old niece were in their spring wagon returning home from a shopping trip in Mulhall. During the trip home, Sam and Will Martin stopped the Hulls. The Martins were intent on settling the score.

Hull offered the boys ten dollars, which they refused. Instead they gave Hull the choice of leaving the country in five days or raising $150, to be left with their pal Clarence Simmons' wife by the end of the week. Hull objected, saying he'd have to sell his farm to raise that kind of money. Sam then threatened to dynamite their house while they slept, saying, "We'll blow your family to hell!"[1]

Mrs. Hull begged them to leave her family alone. The little girl became frightened and took off running down the road. Mrs. Hull called the Martins cowards, but the boys just laughed and repeated their threats.

The Hulls found their niece a mile and a half away and returned home to consider their options. The following day, Hull tried to increase his mortgage by $150, but the bank turned him down. The banker advised Hull to have the Martins arrested, but Hull replied that the Mulhall constable was intimidated by the boys. The banker then recommended the county attorney. Hull visited the attorney, who prepared an extortion complaint, but in the end Hull was afraid to sign it.

The county attorney authorized the sheriff to arrest the Martins. Deputies Charles E. Carpenter and Joe Reynolds were dispatched, with Hull as a guide, to the Martin place. When Hull and the officers arrived at 5 A.M. on May 24, the Martins weren't home. A neighbor claimed he had seen them earlier riding toward the Simmons place. They reached the Simmons place around daybreak, and the deputies knocked on the front door.

Mrs. Simmons answered. The deputies informed her that they had arrest warrants for the Martins and asked if they were there. Clarence Simmons appeared and called up the stairs to Sam, saying that two deputy sheriffs wanted to see him and Will.

After a moment, the deputies heard the back door open and realized the Martins were getting away. The two officers rushed to the back of the house and ordered the brothers to halt. Sam and Will responded by shooting at the deputies. Deputy Reynolds returned fire with a shotgun and downed Will. Carpenter exchanged fire with the fleeing Sam, wounding him, but not badly enough to prevent his escape on horseback. In the meantime, Hull had abandoned the team and wagon and was nowhere to be found.

The officers loaded up the wounded Will Martin and took him to the doctor. An *Oklahoma State Capital* reporter interviewed Will and asked him why he had resisted arrest. He responded, "I'd rather have died than been caught."[2]

Sheriff Rinehart and a posse searched for Sam without success. Sam had secretly escaped to the home of a friend, where he remained hidden until his wound healed. On July 23, a grand jury failed to indict Will, and he was released. He disappeared from the area.

Following the Arkansas River northwest, the Martins drifted to western Oklahoma and Kansas and robbed a series of small stores. In the fall of 1902, they turned up in Prowers County, Colorado, at the Salvation Army Colony of Amity.

Near Amity, in the town of Holly, they fell in with a local desperado, Will M. "Indian Bill" Smith. Smith recruited the Martins for a robbery of a store and post office in nearby Carlton. The three men stole $60.12 in money orders, the contents of the cash drawers, and $20 in change. The clerk recognized Indian Bill, and within an hour a manhunt was underway.

A warrant for Sam and Will Martin was forwarded to U.S. Marshal Bill Fossett of Oklahoma Territory (O.T.) in Guthrie with a $100 reward. The Martins, now fugitives, were reportedly next observed in the Texas Panhandle, No Man's Land, and even Albuquerque, New Mexico. A week before the federal warrants from Denver arrived at the marshal's office in Guthrie, the Martins turned up in Hennessey, O.T.

On March 2, 1903, the southbound train was three hours late arriving in Hennessey. Shortly after the train departed for Kingfisher at 2:30 A.M., three armed men entered the depot waiting room. They robbed the agent of $8.35 and ordered him to open the safe, which he was unable to do. One of the bandits retrieved a crow bar and hammer from a tool shed and attempted to break open the safe.

Several bystanders were held at gunpoint in the waiting room and recognized the bandits as the Martins. While struggling unsuccessfully with the safe, the gang member on guard outside was heard to call out, "Halt!" This command was followed by a shot and a scream.

August "Gus" Cravatt, a young black man, twenty years old, had been shot while innocently returning a lantern he had borrowed from the station. Unaware of the robbery in progress, Cravatt didn't take the order to halt seriously and was shot in the right leg.

The commotion was heard by a night watchman named Bevard,

who came around a corner of the City Hotel, where he was spotted and fired upon by the outlaws. Bevard returned fire but got off only two rounds before his pistol jammed. He ducked behind a telephone pole and tried to unjam the gun. Four shots splintered into the pole before the other two outlaws emerged from the station for a hasty departure. The three bandits rode hard into the night. Their victim, Gus Cravatt, soon died from severe hemorrhage.

At daybreak, U.S. Deputy Marshal Bill Holt and Sheriff E. H. Shumate organized a large posse that was soon on the Martins' trail. Another posse set out from Guthrie, led by U.S. Marshal Fossett himself. The Martins managed to stay ahead of the posses by stealing fresh horses along their way.

On March 5, a wagonload of armed farmers stumbled onto the outlaws' camp near Mulhall and exchanged shots with them. The Martins quickly withdrew, and Fossett again picked up the chase. Near Marshall, Fossett's posse discovered the gang and exchanged fire for around twenty minutes. Again, the gang slipped away into the night.

Needing fresh horses and food, the Martins approached a farmer's house and posed as officers searching for themselves. The farmer pried open the nailed doors of his barn (a precaution against the outlaws) and was forced to hitch a team to his buggy. The farmer's wife was forced to hand over the spareribs she'd prepared for dinner, and the gang was off again.

Fossett and his posse "got the trail by means of sparerib bones which the men threw from the buggy, and a wobbly track left by one wheel of the vehicle..."[3] Muddy roads forced them to abandon the wagon, and they resumed their flight on horseback. Fossett and his men turned over the chase to the Garfield and Kingfisher county posses.

On Saturday morning it was discovered that the gang had spent the previous night with a farmer just five miles from Hennessey. The chase resumed, and the outlaws headed northwest to Woods County.

Late Saturday evening on March 7, Sheriff Oates and his posse came upon the Martins encamped near Isabella, and a twenty-minute gun battle ensued. The outlaws again escaped into the darkness, stole five horses the next morning, and continued northwest.

They were not spotted again until the end of March, riding

along Wolf Creek, near Gage in Woodward County. Two cattle in-
spectors and a deputy sheriff chased the gang into the Panhandle of
Texas, near the town of Canadian. The sheriff of Hemphill County
joined the pursuit, but the elusive Martins disappeared.

Marshal Fossett summed up the chase: "They have stolen fifty
horses since the Hennessey robbery; fully thirty teams have been
tired out by officers—ten teams by myself and my deputies."[4]
Sheriff Carpenter eloquently described the chase: "the damnedest
manhunt in the territory's history."[5]

CHAPTER X

THE MURDERING MARTINS

The Martin gang lay low for several weeks following the great chase. The authorities kept the homes of the Martins and Clarence Simmons under close surveillance, vowing to bring the gang to justice. But the Martins avoided their old haunts and turned up instead in the Osage Nation.

On Sunday, June 14, at around noon, the gang resurfaced on the road between Pawhuska and Bartlesville. About three miles southwest of Bartlesville, the road ran along Liza Creek between two hills. It was here that the outlaws concealed themselves in the heavy cover and waited for unsuspecting travelers. They were in need of fresh mounts, as usual, but this Sunday the gang apparently wanted plenty of stock from which to make their selections.

Shortly after noon, a man named Watson became the first victim when the Martins surprised him and ordered him off his horse at gunpoint. He complied and was led off and placed under guard by one of the gang. Fred Keeler of Bartlesville was the next victim, and he joined Watson with his buggy and team.

Former U.S. deputy marshal Frank Ware and his wife drove by in their buggy in the midafternoon on the way to Pawhuska. When the outlaws ordered them to stop, Ware realized he had fifty dollars in his pocket. He threw up his hands while letting the money drop to the bottom of the buggy. His wife carefully picked up the money and hid it in her hair.

The outlaws didn't see the fifty dollars, but they did recognize Ware as a former officer and stole his watch as a souvenir. As the afternoon wore on, more and more people were systematically stopped and led off to the holding area. One of the victims, Nellie Johnstone Cannon, reported the incident as follows:

> One beautiful Sunday afternoon... as a picnic party composed of Keeler, Johnstone, Bopst, Beattie and Bixler families was returning from a day in the Osage, we were halted by a band of outlaws...We were all quite surprised, and of course considerably frightened... Three bandits... were endeavoring to procure some good saddle horses upon which to make their getaway.
>
> As it took several hours to go through this process of elimination and select the horses... quite a large group of people had assembled-all traffic from both directions being detained by the bandits.[1]

A farmer with a load of hay drove up, but when the Martins stopped him they were unable to get the wagon off the road, so it served as a roadblock. When around one hundred people had been detained, the outlaws began their selection of the three best mounts.

The team of sorrels pulling Fred Keeler's buggy were among the finest animals, but they had never been ridden. Undeterred, the Martins attempted unsuccessfully to ride them, and the crowd was treated to a wild exhibition of bronco busting. Keeler mischievously suggested that the boys use spurs because the horses were used to them. This resulted in the outlaws being thrown all the harder and threats to shoot Keeler for his advice.

Finally, after six or seven hours, the outlaws selected three horses and released their captives. The *Bartlesville Examiner* later noted that "The holdup part took more strongly of a whimsical caper of drunken cowboys than it did of a raid by frontier bandits."[2]

That evening the gang camped in a hollow near Pawhuska. Rancher Clark Riley and his men passed through the hollow while moving cattle, and they were forced to feed the gang.

The citizens of the Osage believed that the bandits were planning to rob the bank in Pawhuska, where money for the Osage payments was held. The *Osage Journal* commented: "Pawhuska would be perhaps the hardest town in the territory for a daylight robbery [because] of the location of the streets surrounding the bank and the large number of people who carry guns."[3]

Haines and Warren Bennett quickly mobilized and scoured the countryside in search of the Martins. But once again, the slippery outlaws vanished without a trace. The Osage swarmed with a small army of lawmen and bounty hunters, lured by the rapidly accumulating reward offers. Haines and Bennett joined the long list of officers who had been frustrated by the Martins, but the lawmen of the Osage were destined to have another fateful encounter with the outlaws.

Chapter XI

Shootout at Wooster Mound

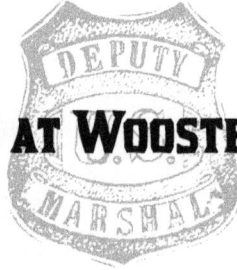

The Martin gang next appeared in Woods County at a small farming community known as Hopeton. On July 2, three men rode into town and hitched their horses outside the general store and post office. Two of the men entered the store while a third remained outside. The two Martins pulled their pistols and forced the storeowner and his assistant to empty the safe and cash drawer. They collected over $100.

As they were finishing up, the third man outside called out, "Halt!" which was followed by a rifle shot. One of the brothers stepped outside to help take shots at a rapidly receding buggy. Before leaving, each bandit "helped himself to a new hat and shirt" and threatened to blow the heads off the store occupants if they left the store in the next twenty minutes.[1]

The description of the bandits, which the storeowner gave the next day in Alva, matched that of the Hennessey and Osage robbers. Sheriff Oates organized a posse, and they trailed them southeasterly before losing them. The evening of July 7, the gang was next reported near Geary, on the Blaine–Canadian county border.

Geary was a rough-and-tumble farming and cattle community with an ample supply of saloons. City Marshal John Cross and his assistant J. D. Wellborn were the only law in Geary. Cross also had a deputy's commission under Canadian County Sheriff John Ozmun.

The evening of July 6, a Geary resident intercepted three heavily armed men crossing the North Canadian River, and another farmer met the trio on the way to town. The next day, Marshal Cross finished his evening rounds at 11 P.M. and headed for home. About 4 A.M. his horse wandered in riderless. The horse had been shot in the eye and the nose. Alarmed, Cross's wife telephoned to Geary, and a search for the marshal was begun.

Within an hour, the marshal's body was discovered in an oat field, a half-mile south of town, with a gunshot wound to the abdomen. Remains of a fire where three men had camped were found near the Cross home. Apparently, Cross had spotted the campfire on his way home and stopped to investigate. He was probably shot from his horse, accounting for the animal's wounds. Cross's badge and watch were missing.

Sheriff Ozmun rode to Geary to investigate and learned about the three strangers who had been seen the night before. It was later believed that they were "casing the banks" in preparation for a robbery. The three matched the descriptions of the Martins and Clarence Simmons.

Ozmun and a posse of thirty men set out after the gang, who were believed to be headed for the Wichita Mountains. On July 8, Governor Ferguson offered a reward of $500 for the Martins, and by July 10 additional rewards brought the grand total to $1,350.

A dispatch from Lawton on July 17 revealed that approximately 200 lawmen were scouring Comanche County for the outlaws. But as usual, the Martins escaped. Nothing was heard until August 4, when a planned train robbery in Noble County was canceled due to the presence of guards on the train. The gang fled east toward the Arkansas River.

Bennett and Wiley Haines became alert as the Martins neared the Osage. They patrolled the eastern border of the reservation for several days but found no sign of the gang. The next few days were quiet, but on August 7, the lawmen were fairly certain their quarry was at hand.

Numerous newspapers recorded the gun battle at Wooster Mound. The *Bartlesville Examiner, Hominy News, Guthrie Daily Leader, Oklahoma City Times,* and other newspapers all relate the same basic story, but some details conflict. This is not surprising, since papers of the times were often prone to sensationalism and unsubstantiated claims. For example, several newspaper accounts claimed that associates of Wiley Haines stated that he had pursued Jesse James in the Osage. Since Haines was only twenty-one and living in California at the time of James' death, this seems unlikely.

Haines himself left no written account of the gun battle with the Martins at Wooster Mound, so historians are left to reconstruct the most accurate version. One of the more credible versions appears in the *Guthrie Daily Leader* of August 11, 1903. Excerpts from this account were reprinted in the *Oklahoma City Times* of 1921. Warren Bennett, a participant in the gun battle, was quoted extensively in these sources.

Bennett's story begins when the officers received notification in Pawhuska on Friday evening, August 7, by the occupants of an Indian camp. The presence of some armed men in the vicinity matched the description of the Martins. The following afternoon, the officers in Pawhuska learned that the outlaws were camped about eight miles southeast of town. The outlaws were hidden behind a knoll, in a deep ravine, surrounded by a canyon. The Guthrie paper account claimed that "the camp had evidently been the hiding place of the gang on more than a few times."[2]

Warren Bennett, Haines, and Constable Henry Majors set out on horseback from Pawhuska for the camp, reaching it around 6 P.M. The camp was near a place known as Wooster's Mound, a rise on the banks of Birch Creek. The officers dismounted a short distance from the camp so as to approach it undetected. Cautiously, the three officers moved to within one hundred yards. They spotted two men cooking dinner over a small fire near a pile of saddles and equipment. A third man guarded the horses nearby.

The three lawmen decided to split up, with Majors approaching from the left, Haines from the right, and Bennett headed directly toward the camp. One of the outlaw's horses snorted and alerted the bandits, who grabbed for their guns and came up shooting.

Sam Martin positioned himself behind the saddles and opened up with a rifle as his brother Will dashed for the creek. Bennett and Haines advanced, but Majors somehow became separated. Haines fired at the fleeing Will Martin, hitting him in the leg and slowing him down. A second shot caught Will in the mouth, exiting at the back of his neck and killing him instantly.

Bennett and Haines charged the camp in the face of Sam Martin's fire. One of Sam's bullets struck Haines in the right shoulder and chest, wounding him severely and knocking him from his feet. Bennett, by this time, was upon Sam and forced the wounded outlaw to surrender. Meanwhile, the third bandit, Clarence Simmons, was making a hasty retreat. Haines got a good look at him as he fled. Simmons galloped away while Bennett was subduing Sam Martin.

As rapidly as the gun battle had begun, it was over. The shootout lasted less than a minute, during which time twenty-seven shots were fired. Will Martin lay dead, Sam was fatally wounded, and Haines was critically wounded. Bennett pursued Simmons for about an hour before giving up.

Some Osage Indians from a nearby camp heard the shooting and came over to offer assistance. Haines and the wounded Sam Martin were loaded into the back of a spring wagon and transported over the bumpy road to the doctor's office in Pawhuska.

Sam's wounds were rapidly determined to be fatal, but he remained conversant to the end. The doctor turned his attention to Haines and recommended a general anesthetic before operating to remove the bullet. Haines refused the anesthetic, eyeing the dangerous outlaw who was still alive and in the same room with him.

Haines held his pistol in his left hand and pointed it at Sam Martin while the doctor extracted bullet fragments from his shoulder. Haines wanted to be certain that there would be no chance for another Martin escape. After the painful surgery, Haines was bandaged and Sam was made comfortable for his last hours on earth.

When the doctor saw that the end was near for Sam, he sent for a priest. The priest arrived and gave Sam his last rites, then turned and began on Wiley. When Haines realized what was happening, he became agitated and exclaimed to the priest, "Get the hell out of here! I'm not dead yet!"[3]

Bennett collected the gang's plunder of the gang, which included three stolen horses, saddles and bridles, two rifles, four revolvers, 1,000 rounds of ammunition, and the latest style belts and pouches for carrying extra cartridges. Two horses were identified as among those stolen in the Bartlesville holdup.

A search of Will Martin's pockets revealed a silver watch that had belonged to City Marshal John Cross. Cross's badge was recovered from Will's saddlebag.

As Haines lay critically wounded, word was sent to Hominy,

and Sarah and their ten-year-old son, John, drove by buggy to Pawhuska. Wiley managed to hang on, and Sam Martin lingered until Sunday night at 9 P.M., when he finally died. Sam confessed to many of the crimes attributed to the gang, including the depot robbery and shooting of Gus Cravatt in Hennessey, the robbery of over 100 people outside Bartlesville, and the Hopeton Post Office robbery. Sam also confirmed that the third man who had escaped at Wooster Mound was Clarence Simmons.

Sam boasted, "We've robbed more people than any gang in history. Why in one afternoon we robbed more'n a hundred." He bragged that rewards for his capture totaled over $7,000. Rewards aggregating $12,000 had been offered for the gang, dead or alive. But as the end drew near, Sam took the opportunity to repent with the classic statement, "I guess I have been on the wrong trail."[4]

The *Guthrie Daily Leader* proclaimed, "The Martin Gang was considered one of the most daring and death-defying gangs that have ever been chased by officers."[5]

Warren Bennett transported the bodies of the Martin brothers to the train station in Ralston, where he met Marshals Willits and Jacobson, who helped him transfer the bodies to Guthrie. The bodies arrived Tuesday morning and were taken to the Patterson Funeral Home to be prepared for burial. The *Oklahoma State Capital* commented on their arrival: "After years of running amok... committing innumerable robberies and staining their hands with human blood... Sam and Will Martin are lying side by side in the dead house, with eyes closed, hands tied across their breasts and ghastly wounds where their young lives went out in a hopeless struggle to try to take by force what could much easier be won by honest toil."[6]

The corpses were placed on slabs for public viewing, and hundreds of people filed past during the afternoon. The seventy-year-old father of Clarence Simmons came to make certain that one of the dead outlaws was not his son. He left the scene "sobbing bitterly."[7]

Marshal Fossett telegraphed the dead men's father in Comanche regarding the disposition of the bodies. A reply was not received from Luther Martin until August 13. The message said simply, "Am unable to take care of the bodies. Dispose of them according to law."[8]

The *Oklahoma State Capitol* could not resist editorializing by responding, "They have already been disposed of according to law... they will now be disposed of according to custom."[9]

Later that day, in the potter's field of Guthrie's Summit View Cemetery, the Martins joined their comrades who had fallen along the outlaw trail.

By August 17, Warren Bennett was able to communicate to Marshal Fosset's office in Guthrie, "Wiley Haines is improving, about 85 percent of the bullet particles having been extracted... He is practically out of danger."[10]

Marshal Fossett responded:

> My experience with the Martins, in all cases, has been that they gave their victims no show whatever, and no doubt would have done the same with you and Haines had they any warning.... As they were equally matched, three on each side, it should be a warning to all lawbreakers in our territory to keep clear of officers...
>
> I am proud and the territory should be and no doubt is proud of such officers, and to know that I have not been disappointed, believing that if my deputies got an even show with any band of outlaws they would come out victorious....
>
> I regret very much Wiley Haines being wounded, but thank God, it is no worse... Do me a kindness to have everything done for him that can be, and if you can't get proper attention and medical aid where he is, have him brought to Guthrie to my house and taken good care of at my expense.[11]

While Haines recovered, he received many telegrams, letters, and personal calls from friends and associates congratulating him for wiping out the Martin gang. U.S. District Attorney Horace Speed sent Wiley a special commendation, which read in part, "No better stroke for law and order in the territory was ever made than in the wiping out of the vicious Martins."

Governor Ferguson arranged for Warren Bennett to be paid two-thirds of the reward offered for the murder of City Marshal John Cross. Bennett split the money with Haines and Henry Majors. Several leads regarding Clarence Simmons were pursued but quickly ended. It would be eighteen years before Haines crossed paths with the treacherous Simmons again.

By late October, Haines had recovered enough to resume his duties. Within days of returning to work, Haines captured outlaw Walter McClain, who had escaped in the famous jailbreak led by Bill Doolin in 1896.

Simmons was finally apprehended in 1919 in Booneville, Missouri. Simmons had escaped to Jacksonville, Florida, where he had worked "as an everyday businessman" as Jackson J. Smith (not the most imaginative alias). Simmons and his second wife appeared in Booneville in late March. He had come to see his new grand-daughter.

Simmons had abandoned his wife and daughter when he fled Oklahoma in 1903. His first wife divorced him, and their daughter had grown up, married, and had a child of her own. The Simmons family had lived in Booneville before moving to Oklahoma in the 1890s but was still known in the area. Some of Clarence Simmons' old acquaintances recognized "Mr. Smith," and this resulted in his arrest by Booneville Chief of Police J. R. Miller.

Simmons was returned to Oklahoma and stood trial in Kingfisher County in October of 1920 for the murder of Gus Cravatt. But the witnesses to the crime could not positively iden-tify Simmons, and he was acquitted of the crime. Problems identi-fying Simmons also resulted in no charges being filed in the Hopeton robbery and the murder of Marshal John Cross.

But Haines had no problems identifying Simmons as the outlaw who had escaped from the deadly gun battle at Wooster Mound. A wide search was conducted for material witnesses in the case. The trial attracted many notable lawmen, including former U.S. mar-shals Chris Madsen and Bill Tilghman, along with around 100 wit-nesses for the government.

Before the trial got underway, the government's star witness, Wiley Haines, appeared at the federal building in Oklahoma City and displayed to curious onlookers the bullet fragments that had been ex-tracted from his shoulder wound acquired in the 1903 gun battle.

The *Daily Oklahoman* praised Haines as a member of "the finest force of law enforcers the world had ever seen—the old time United States Marshals."[12] The Simmons case got underway on January 28, 1921. The *Oklahoman* set the stage for the dramatic trial with the following description:

> Across the polished mahogany tables, beneath the ornate bar of the court, three men faced each other... Jackson J. Smith, the common-place name given the prisoner, and Wiley Haines and Henry Majors, the latter now a police chief... Simmons, or Smith, has only his at-

torney and wife who, until his arrest, had never heard of the alleged offenses of his youth. Warren Bennett and lesser witnesses to the battle have gone their ways... The meeting bridges an eighteen year gap in the course of law enforcement in a land which has seen in that time the last wild west go through fast grinding mills of present day social culture. It marks the final efforts of the United States government to bring its law to bear upon one of the most notorious bandit organizations which ever infested Oklahoma before marble courtrooms were dreamed of.[13]

A good deal of evidence was introduced by the defense, trying to establish Simmons' supposed residence in Florida before and during the time of the Martins' rampage. Majors was unable to positively identify Simmons, but Wiley was certain. As the *Daily Oklahoman* reported: "Though 62 years of age, a bit wrinkled now from his years in the open, with a stoop in his shoulders that was missing in the stirring days of eighteen years ago, his clear, blue eyes still gaze out in their old-time fire, taking in all there is of men and things."[14]

The jury, however, was unable to reach a verdict, and they were dismissed. Simmons was released on bond, and the case was set for rehearing but ultimately languished in the courts for years. When Haines died in 1928, the government lost its star witness, and the case against Simmons was dropped.

CHAPTER XII

WARREN BENNETT

Two years following the famous shootout with the Martins, Warren Bennett died from a pulmonary hemorrhage. Bennett's death at the age of thirty-five was a great shock. Haines had lost a good friend and a valued colleague. He and Sarah had even named their youngest son Warren Bennett Haines in his honor.

Haines succeeded Bennett as chief of the Osage Indian Police until the system was abolished with statehood in 1907. A few anecdotes about Bennett's abbreviated career have survived. The *Osage Journal* of July 18, 1901, recorded: "Our friend Warren Bennett was in town one day last week. He gave Washington Ellington a free trip to Pawnee. He came back again and took Sam Hopper in and gave him a free trip to Pawhuska for boot leggin' whiskey. Warren is a hummer. He keeps things a moving. If we had a few more like him this foolishness would stop."[1]

Another amusing anecdote, which features Bennett, appeared in E.D. Nix's *Oklahombres*. While it cannot be verified, it does illustrate the daring and courage that Bennett was known for:

> One of my young deputies, Warren Bennett, made a most remarkable capture when he found an overcame Rolla Kapp, a gigantic cattle thief. Bennett had trailed him for several days, but the outlaw had succeeded in eluding him. The young deputy learned the location of the outlaw's home and found it on the desolate side of a sand

hill about twenty miles from Pawhuska. The deputy watched the house for a whole day and until about midnight, and not a soul stirred about the place. Unrolling his blankets and hobbling his horse, Bennett crept up to the house and lay down on the porch before the entrance to sleep. The morning air was cool and pleasant and the officer was sleeping peacefully when he suddenly sensed danger and was awakened. Rolla Kapp, the cattle thief, stood over him, his pistol in his hand. Bennett gazed at him a second through half-closed eyelids, then with a lightning movement threw his blanket aside, drew his gun and shot the outlaw through the right wrist.

Kapp's pistol fell rattling to the floor of the porch and the cow thief quickly grabbed his other forty-five with his left hand. Bennett shot him through the left arm before the tip of his gun left the holster. All of this happened so quickly that Bennett still lay upon the floor of the porch on his back, while the outlaw stood writhing in pain above him.

The deputy sprang quickly to his feet and snapped the handcuffs on Kapp's wrists.[2]

Kapp was convicted and received a sentence of five years at the penitentiary in Leavenworth. Bennett was congratulated on the arrest by Marshal Nix, to which Bennett replied, "Why Marshal, there was nothing extraordinary about it... when I looked up and saw that cow thief standing over me with his gun in his hand, I knew it was me or him. I sure didn't want it to be me."[3]

Throughout Haines' career in the Osage, he worked closely with the various representatives of the U.S. Department of Interior. Indian Agents like Isaac T. Gibson and Major Laban Miles were known for their integrity and fairness in dealing with the Osage. One Osage agent, Frank Frantz, was appointed territorial governor of Oklahoma in 1906 while still an agent.

As a young man, Frantz had made the Cherokee Outlet Land Run in 1893. He settled in Enid. When the war with Spain broke out in 1898, he joined the U.S. Volunteer Cavalry as a lieutenant. The regiment became known as the "Rough Riders," and Frantz served under Lt. Col. Theodore Roosevelt. Frantz distinguished himself in one of the charges up San Juan Hill, when he assumed command of his company after the company commander was killed. Roosevelt praised Frantz's valiant conduct and promoted him to captain.

Roosevelt did not forget the young Captain Frantz after the war. He appointed him the last territorial governor of Oklahoma in 1906. Frantz became the youngest executive of any state or territory in the Union. Six months after Frantz took office, Congress passed the Omnibus Statehood Bill, which became the enabling act for Oklahoma and Indian Territory.

This legislation called for the election of delegates to a constitutional convention. Ninety-nine of the 112 delegates elected were Democrats. They convened at Guthrie on November 20, 1906. They adjourned on July 16, 1907, and a ratification of the constitution and first state election on September 17, 1907. In that election, Frantz ran as the Republican candidate for governor against Democrat Charles Haskell. Wiley campaigned for his former colleague, but Haskell carried the election 137,579 to 110,293. Frantz's brief administration ended November 16, 1907.

Wiley, Sarah, and son John (in World War I uniform), 1918.

Wiley Haines and daughter Ironica (on arm), about 1920.

Wiley G. Haines

*Colt .44-40 (above) and badge presented to Wiley Haines,
1890, Oklahoma City; other pistol presented by Osage Tribe.*

"Tools of the trade" of Wiley G. Haines, handcuffs and leg-irons.

Standing, left to right—Wiley, Sarah, Mary, Vera, Wiley Jr., Elma, unknown, Ironica. Kneeling—Virgil, Warren, Kenneth Haines (son of Wiley Jr.) on Warren's knee.

Sarah Haines in front of Wiley and Sarah's home, 1921,
a home with fifteen rooms to accommodate nine children. Hominy, Oklahoma.

Old Osage Indian Agency, Pawhuska, Oklahoma.

USDM Wiley G. Haines, third from left, with Texas Rangers during Prohibition.

DEPARTMENT OF THE INTERIOR
INDIAN SERVICE
WASHINGTON

JUL 1 1913 , 19

Whereas, reposing special confidence in the integrity and ability of

Wiley G. Haines

I hereby commission him a Deputy Special Officer to assist in suppressing the liquor traffic among the Indians and authorize him to fulfill

the duties of that office under authority of law (34 Stat. L. 1015; Public 454, Mar. 3, 1911, and Public 335, Aug. 24, 1912), and as authorized by the Department of the Interior.

This commission expires JUN 30 191 , 19 unless sooner revoked.

[signature]
Chief Special Officer.

Affirmed:
[signature]
Commissioner of Indian Affairs.

_____
Signature of Officer.

Negro lynched in Osage.

Early 1920s parade, Main Street, Hominy, Oklahoma.

Marshal Wiley G. Haines and Pawnee Indian who took place of Pawnee Bill, who was ill at that time.

Campaign picture of Marshal Haines, taken in 1928 for Osage County sheriff's race.
He died of a heart attack shortly afterward, at sixty-eight years of age.

VOTE
FOR
WILEY
G.
HAINES
FOR YOUR
SHERIFF

———

A Man that Knows How to Enforce
the Law without Tolerating
Snitches

———

A DEMOCRAT
OVER 30 YEARS IN OSAGE COUNTY
SUBJECT TO AUGUST 7th PRIMARY

WILEY G. HAINES

CANDIDATE FOR

Sheriff of Osage County

Subject to the Democratic
Primary, August 4, 1914

HOMINY, OKLA.

POSTAL CARD ONE CENT.

United States America

THIS SIDE IS FOR ADDRESS ONLY.

STRAYED OR STOLEN.

One Light Sorrell Mare Eight years old, about Fourteen hands high
with the following on hip [----]: Mare with foal. A liberal reward
will be paid for her return or information regarding her whereabouts.

A. J. FARRINGTON,

Oklahoma City, Oct. 31, 1892.

POSTAL CARD - ONE CENT.

UNITED STATES OF AMERICA

THIS SIDE IS FOR THE ADDRESS ONLY.

Wiley Hains
Hominy Post
Osage Nation
O. T.

$50.00 Reward!

STOLEN, from Pawnee, on night of July 30, one small liver-colored Irish Setter, about 18 months old. Dog is listed on tax rolls at $50.00.

A reward of $50.00 will be paid for capture of thief and return of dog to owner, W. P. PATTON, or to

JOHN CRISMON, Sheriff,
PAWNEE, O. T.

$20.00 Reward.

$10.00 of the above reward will be paid for the recovery of a saddle taken from my barn, on Jim Brown's farm, 12 miles west of Claremore, on May 24, 1901, The saddle was of Billy Campbell's make—being branded with the picture of a camel and "Billy" written on picture; 3-4 rig, cantle and horn uncovered, steel fork, heavy tree, and made of first-class California leather.

$10.00 will also be paid for the arrest and conviction of thief.   J. F. JOHNSON,
                                        Collinsville, I. T.

POSTAL CARD - ONE CENT.

UNITED STATES OF AMERICA.

THIS SIDE IS FOR THE ADDRESS ONLY.

Postmaster

Hominy

STOLEN!--$25 Reward.

From Bartles' Picnic Ground, Bartlesville, on the night of July 4th, 1901, a 7-year-old mare, color between brown and bay, weighs about 950 pounds, right ear been cut with wire and tip turned back, unbranded.

Also a new roll saddle, numbered 2245, weighs 26 pounds, iron stirrups; plain fenders, skirt and jockey.

A reward of $25.00 will be paid for the return of the property or information leading to its recovery.

Address E. H. SMITH, Dewey,

or J. R. PERKINS, Bartlesville.

Wire information to

John W. Wilson, deputy marshal, Bartlesville, I. T.

STRAYED OR STOLEN

sorrel

One Bay Horse about seven years old, weighing about 800 pounds, blaze faced and has a white spot on the back, near tail.   No brand.

$20.00 REWARD

will be paid for information leading to recovery.

MA-SAH-MUM-PAH

Bug Creek Camp, 12 miles west of Hominy, Okla.

STOLEN.

From J. K. Crutchfield, Inola, I. T., one dark bay horse, spot in forehead, light wire cut under fetlock on left front foot. Sixteen hands high, 5 years old, weight about 1100 pounds.

$75 Reward.

$25 for horse and $50 for thief. Liberal reward for information. Address

CAP HARRIS, Pres.,

ALBERT LEWIS, Sec'y,

Lodge No. 34, A. H. T. A., Inola, I. T.

POSTAL CARD - ONE CENT.

UNITED STATES OF AMERICA.

THIS SIDE IS FOR THE ADDRESS ONLY.

Stolen!--$15 Reward.

On Saturday night March 17, a horse of the following description was stolen from Henry Bascom: Dark sorrel, weighing about 900 pounds, 15 hands high, star in forehead with white strip running down to nose. Also a plain leather saddle with wooden stirrup and a riding bridle from R. S. Hagan. The thief was a dark complected young man weighing about 125 pounds and giving the name of Jim Rogers. $15 reward will be paid for the arrest of thief and return of property.

Address: Henry Bascom or R. S. Hagan,

Bartlesville, I. T.

$60 REWARD.

Stolen, from B. R. McLain, on Fish creek, eight miles southeast of Bartlesville, on Sunday night, June 30, a set of double harness described as follows: Light work harness, plain finish, used about 18 months, three butts of tugs next to hames have been lately repaired, concord hames and new breast-straps, butt britchen, one blind bridle and one open, one new hitch rein and one old.

The above reward will be paid by Fish Creek Lodge No. 286, Anti-Horsethief association—$40 for capture and conviction of thief and $20 for return of harness.

J. H. GOODWIN, President Fish Creek A. H. T. A.

B. R. McLain, Secretary pro tem.

Post Office address, Bartlesville, I. T.

POSTAL CARD ONE CENT
United States of America
THIS SIDE IS FOR ADDRESS ONLY

Deply U.S. Marshal
Oklahoma City
O.T.

Stolen
From H. A. Hines one mile south of Dover
Oklahoma on the Evening of the 3rd of November
1892 one ½ Clyde bay mare about 16 hands
high. three year old last spring Bald face
front feet and right hind foot white. hoops
on front feet striped. Main and tail heavy
and curley. I will give twentyfive dollars
$25 reward for the return of said mare or for
information where she is if it prover
Correct
H. A. Hines

Will Jackson
Horney
a. T.

$50 Reward.

STOLEN:—On Tuesday night, June 11, one dark brown or black horse, six years old, 15½ hands high, weight 1000 pounds, blind in right eye. mane was at one time roached, but at present is 7 or 8 inches long. No brands. Horse has what is commonly termed a hog back.

Will pay $10.00 for information that will lead to the recovery of horse, or $50 for return of horse and capture of thief. Address,   **Dr. Lankford**

or

City Marshal,

Tulsa, Ind. Ter

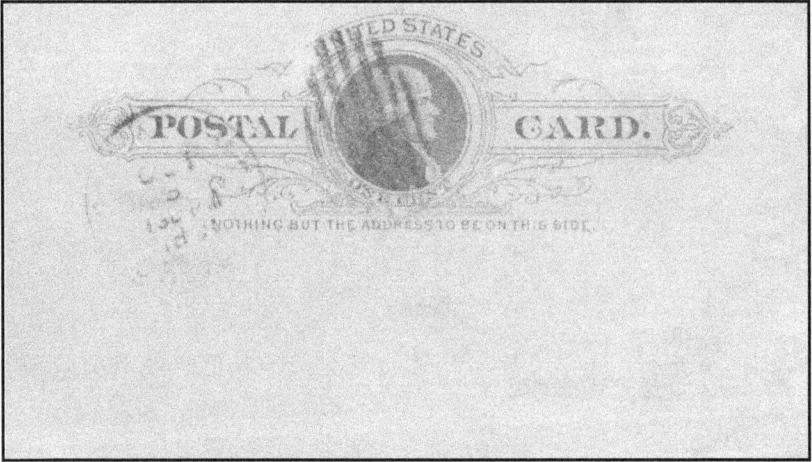

STOLEN

On the night of October 1st., at 11:30 p. m., at Tecumseh,
One bright Bay Horse six years old. Has white spot on
his forehead the size of a dollar. Is about 15½ hands high;
a scar on the left side of his tail in the shape of a V. Is
fresh shod in front.

A REWARD of $25.00 for the return of the horse and
$25.00 for the arrest of the thief.

Address,

JOHN T. CARR,

Oklahoma City, O. T.

Wiley Haines' name inscribed on Register Cliff, Wyoming, along the Oregon Trail.

Dedication of Oklahoma Historical Marker of "The Battle of Wooster Mound,"
October 28, 1995.
Left to right—Chief Deputy Marshal Robin Fagala; Dr. Joe Haines, Jr.; Warren B.
Haines, last surviving son of Wiley Haines; Joe Haines, Sr.; Dee Cordry; Glenn
Shirley; U.S. Marshal Northern District Oklahoma Jim Hughes.

CHAPTER XIII

LYNCHING IN THE OSAGE

Four months before Indian Territory united with Oklahoma Territory to become the forty-sixth state in the Union, the first recorded lynching in the Osage Nation occurred. The lynching was also only the fourth reported in the territory. While it is difficult to confirm lynchings, it is a fact that "mob law" was a rarity in Indian Territory.

Justice in Indian Territory was administered by a small army of U.S. deputy marshals. Many were under the jurisdiction of "Hanging Judge" Isaac Parker in Fort Smith, Arkansas. During his tenure, Parker's courts lost sixty-five deputy marshals killed in the line of duty, a testament to the criminal activity of the era. Other marshals in Indian Territory reported to courts in Guthrie and Muskogee.

With such a formidable corps of law-enforcement officers, lynchings were uncommon. The term "lynching" is usually associated with hanging, but almost any form of violent death carried out by a group of private citizens could be called a lynching. The word may be derived from John Lynch Fitz-Stephens, a sixteenth-century Irishman. Fitz-Stephens reportedly hanged his own son for murder while warden of Galway Jail. However, the term can also be traced to a Virginia farmer, Joseph Lynch, who hanged Negroes in the 1780s.

Vigilantism is often associated with lynching in the American

West. Vigilante groups were a more or less organized body that functioned out of necessity due to the absence of law-enforcement agencies. Some vigilante groups, however, did ultimately deteriorate into mobs.

On the evening of July 16, 1907, the Osage Nation experienced its first lynch mob. In the southern part of the reservation, in the town of Osage, a Missouri-Kansas-Texas brakeman, Frank Kelly, discovered a Negro, Frank Bailey, trying to steal a ride on the train. Kelly put Bailey off the train and warned him not to return.

Rather than leaving, Bailey hid in the train yard and waited for a chance to get even with Kelly. Bailey soon spotted Kelly walking down the train atop some boxcars. He allegedly took aim with his pistol and shot Kelly in the chest. Bailey fled, but railroad detective Walter Bare quickly organized a posse, which captured Bailey an hour later one mile east of Osage. The posse returned Bailey to the train depot and held him there until a marshal could arrive and take him into custody.

Meanwhile, Frank Kelly was carried to a hotel, the Osage Inn, where he received medical attention. The doctor pronounced the chest wound critical. Word spread rapidly in the small town about the shooting, and a crowd gathered at the depot. The crowd became increasingly unruly and transformed into a mob when three masked men emerged, declaring that they would take matters into their own hands.

As a Pawhuska newspaper account recorded: "A sort of temporary emotional insanity seized the crowd and they permitted the masked men to take Mr. Coon out and hang him."[1]

The two men guarding Bailey were easily overpowered by the mob, and Bailey was dragged to the town park just east of the railroad yard, where he was strung up to die from strangulation.

Most of the newspaper accounts of the time wholeheartedly supported the act, with the *Hominy News* declaring, "the Negro got his just desserts."[2]

The Pawhuska paper noted that "This affair is to be deplored, but public sympathy is with the lynchers. They create a more profound respect for the law than does rulings of the court."[3] Only in the *Foraker Tribune* did reason prevail when they wrote, "lynch law is all wrong and profitable to no man or community."[4]

Witnesses claimed that fifteen men actively participated in the lynching. There were an estimated thirty witnesses to the crime. U.S. Deputy Marshals John Abernathy, Wiley Haines, and John Freeman investigated the lynching, which resulted in the arrest of three men. Melville G. White, Charles A. Green, and Frank Williams were all charged with the murder of Frank Bailey.

A grand-jury investigation returned an indictment against the three men, but the charges were ultimately dismissed for reasons not found in the court records. Taking into account Bailey's apparent guilt and his race, it is not surprising that the three men did not answer for their crime. Frank Kelly recovered from his wound, and a tragic chapter in the annals of the Osage came to a close.

The vast majority of Haines' confrontations with lawbreakers were nonviolent. While the violent episodes tend to be the most remembered, the nonviolent encounters often best reveal an officer's character.

John, Wiley Haines' eldest son, recalled the story of Haines' barber, an ex–horse thief his father had once sent to prison. In the early 1900s an Osage named Che-sho-hun-kah who lived near Grayhorse reported that five of his horses had been stolen. Even though the thieves had a three-day headstart, Haines was able to track them nearly two hundred miles before overtaking them in the Greenleaf Mountains of the Cherokee country.

In Tulsa, Haines had been joined by Deputy U.S. Marshal H. A. Thompson of the Western District of Indian Territory. A posse independent of the two lawmen was also in pursuit, undoubtedly with plans of hanging the thieves if they caught them first. The thieves were attempting to cross the rain-swollen Arkansas River with the horses when the lawmen rode up on them.

The outlaws were only distinguished as one having black hair and the other having red hair. The black-haired man drew a bead on Haines with his rifle. Before he could shoot, the red-haired man told his partner, "Don't shoot, that's a federal marshal!"

While the black-haired outlaw considered the advice, Haines called out, "It would be better off for you to come with me than for the posse to catch up with you."

The outlaw lowered the rifle. The men gave their names as C. W. Bailey and J. T. Thompson. They were arraigned before the U.S. Commissioner E. N. Yates and pleaded not guilty. Their bond was fixed at $1,000 each, which they were unable to pay. The pair were jailed, tried, convicted, and imprisoned. While in prison, the black-haired outlaw was killed, but the redhead (which was Bailey and which was Thompson is unknown) completed his sentence and eventually returned to Pawhuska, where he worked as a barber.

Young John Haines often accompanied his father to Pawhuska, and they would visit the redheaded barber for a haircut. Invariably, the barber would impress upon young John that his father, Wiley, had saved his life by ending his career as a horse thief.[5]

CHAPTER XIV

THE ABERNATHY BOYS

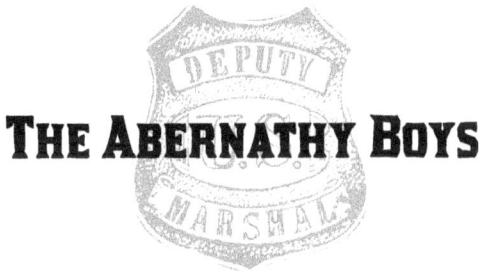

The life of a frontier marshal didn't consist of merely chasing outlaws. Wiley Haines had numerous opportunities to help folks. In 1910 Bud and Temple Abernathy were the recipients of Haines' generosity. The boys' father was U.S. Marshal John R. Abernathy, also known as "Catch 'em Alive" Jack Abernathy for his wolf-hunting exploits.

President Theodore Roosevelt named Abernathy U.S. marshal for Oklahoma in 1906. As noted by writer Glenn Shirley, "Abernathy's appointment was viewed with mixed feelings in Oklahoma. Many felt that Marshal Fossett should have been retained or the post given to one of the "Three Guardsmen"[1] [Madsen, Tilghman, and Thomas].

For field deputies, Abernathy appointed Wiley Haines at Pawhuska, Edward Pregnier at Ponca City, James G. Knox at Enid, James Bourland at Anadarko, Tom S. Walker at Lawton, John P. Jones at Shawnee, and Sheriff Martin at Chandler. Abernathy furthered his cause by naming Chris Madsen as Chief U.S. Deputy Marshal and re-commissioning Bill Tilghman and Heck Thomas.[2]

Marshal Abernathy's two sons, Bud and Temple, aged six and nine, captured the interest of the nation in the spring and summer of 1910. Following in the adventuresome footsteps of their father, Bud and Temple set out on a cross-country trip by horseback from

Oklahoma to Washington, D.C. The summer before their famous journey, the boys had successfully covered over 2,000 miles on their own from Oklahoma to Santa Fe and back.

On April 15, 1910, Bud and Temple set out from their home near Frederick, Oklahoma, on their horses, Sam Bass and Geronimo. Since the boys were both expert horsemen, their father had only four rules for them: 1) never travel on Sundays, 2) never carry more than five dollars to discourage thieves, 3) never ride into water unless they could see the bottom or had help crossing, and 4) never ride more than fifty miles a day, except to reach shelter for themselves and their horses.

The first day, the boys rode to Lawton, where they spent the night in a hotel. The next morning, Bud paid the bill with a check from an account his father had set up for them. The boys later learned that people were not cashing the checks, preferring to keep them as autographed souvenirs.

The boys rode on to Oklahoma City, where they met their father. They spent three days seeing the sights before saying good-bye and beginning their trip in earnest. Each night, the boys either camped or called on friends along their route. Soon they reached the Osage Nation and stopped to rest in Hominy at Wiley Haines' place. The next day as the boys prepared to leave, they encountered their first misfortune of the trip. Temple's horse, Geronimo, went lame. The boys talked the situation over with Haines, and they decided to stay over with him in Hominy an extra day to let the horse rest.

The following day, Geronimo was no better. Haines advised the boys to buy a new horse and took them to a rancher who sold horses. Temple picked out his new mount and paid $85 for the horse and for food for Geronimo. Temple named the horse Wiley Haines to show his appreciation.[3]

The weather turned wet after leaving Hominy as they passed through Pawhuska and across the state line to Coffeyville, Kansas. They then turned east to Joplin and Springfield. East of Springfield, the cold rain turned to deep snow. They finally made it to St. Louis, where they recuperated for a week.

The going was much easier across Illinois and Indiana, and they made good time. By now, news of the journey was in all the papers, prompting large crowds to turn out to greet the boys in every town.

In Cincinnati, they stopped for a day and saw the zoo. In Dayton, Ohio, they met the governor and Wilbur Wright, who gave them a tour of his airplane factory.

Before they left Ohio, Temple became ill with pneumonia and a fever of 103 degrees. They were forced to stop in Cambridge, Ohio, where Temple saw a doctor and spent two days in bed. Temple bounced back, and the boys crossed into West Virginia. Near Wheeling, West Virginia, they became impatient and unwisely broke one of their father's rules.

After waiting an hour for help in crossing a swift-running creek, the boys attempted a crossing on their own. Bud tried the creek first to see if it was safe, and he swam across on Sam Bass. Bud then crossed back over to let Temple cross on the more experienced Sam Bass. Temple made it across without any problem, but the less experienced horse, Wiley Haines, quickly got into difficulty.

Wiley was not a strong swimmer, and he and Bud began drifting with the current. Temple ran along the bank shouting encouragement as Bud urged the horse on. After being swept downstream nearly two hundred yards, Wiley finally found his footing. They made it across, but the brothers had learned the value of their father's advice—the hard way.

The journey through Pennsylvania and Maryland went well. On May 27, 1910, Bud and Temple proudly rode into Washington, D.C. After taking in the sights, the boys put on their suits and headed for the White House to meet President William Howard Taft. Bud thought Taft was "big and jolly, but he didn't play with us like Teddy did."

The last leg of the trip was to New York City for a rendezvous with their father and Teddy Roosevelt, whom they had met on a 1907 hunting trip in Oklahoma. Marshal Abernathy hunted on horseback with greyhounds and would ride the wolves down. While the dogs held the wolf, Abernathy leapt from the saddle and thrust a gloved fist between the animal's jaws. He then grasped the upper jaw with his left hand and tied both jaws together with bailing wire.

Abernathy sold the unharmed wolves to zoos all over the country for five dollars a head. The only time he was injured was in sustaining a wolf bite to the forearm. He debrided the wound with some rusty sheep shears.

The presidential hunting party ranged between the Wichita

Mountains and the Red River for four days, bagging seventeen wolves. Roosevelt roped one wolf, which Abernathy muzzled and carried five miles to camp. The delighted Roosevelt gave a speech before leaving Oklahoma, thanking everyone for "as pleasant a five day outing as any president ever had." Roosevelt praised Abernathy's hunting technique as "a remarkable exhibition of pluck and skill."[4]

The Abernathys were guests of Roosevelt in New York City for several days before starting the journey homeward. To cap the adventure, Marshal Abernathy arranged for Bud and Temple to drive themselves home in a car called a Brush Runabout. The marshal and his driver would follow along in a larger automobile, a Maxwell.

Word of the trip again made the newspapers nationwide. Some criticized Marshal Abernathy as a promoter who exploited his sons. Others believed the trips were merely an extension of the father's flamboyant personality.

After a large farewell luncheon at the Hotel Astor, Bud and Temple pulled out of Times Square on July 6, 1910. Bud concentrated on his driving while Temple waved his hat to the crowd that had come to see them off. By the time they reached Ohio, Bud was an expert driver. In Detroit they visited the factory where the Brush Runabout was produced at the rate of 100 a day.

West of Chicago, the roads deteriorated rapidly. Sometimes they had just rutted trails to follow. Then near-disaster struck near Wellington, Kansas. The Maxwell car Marshal Abernathy was in caught fire. Fortunately, neither he nor the driver were injured and the car was repaired to complete the final leg of the journey.

On July 29, Bud and Temple crossed the Oklahoma border. Their journey east had taken two months and the drive back just three weeks. In all, they had covered over 5,000 miles since leaving in April.

The following year, two promoters promised Bud and Temple $10,000 if they could ride on horseback from coast to coast in sixty days. The boys readily accepted the challenge. On August 11, 1911, Bud and Temple, then eleven and seven, set out from Coney Island, New York with 10,000 spectators cheering them on.

Sam Bass and Wiley Haines were once again their faithful mounts. The rules of the race specified that they could not eat or sleep under a roof during the entire journey. Tragedy struck near Cheyenne, Wyoming, when Sam Bass suddenly died. Bud replaced his old friend, and the boys raced on, completing the 3,619-mile ride in San Francisco. But they arrived just two days past the deadline for winning the $10,000 prize.

Bud and Temple's remarkable rides were feats that most boys could only dream about. Their amazing journeys symbolized the end of one era and the beginning of another. As Robert B. Jackson wrote about the Abernathy boys, "They were in a sense a symbol of what the whole country was going through. It was a time when the horse was being replaced with the automobile. Eventually, the way of life they knew would be totally gone."[5] For a few years, however, Bud and Temple Abernathy had their feet planted firmly in both worlds.

CHAPTER XV

OSAGE REIGN OF TERROR

Near the end of Wiley Haines's career, he assisted in the investigation of a series of murders in Osage County. In the early 1920s, perhaps scores of Osage Indians were murdered in schemes to acquire their fabulous oil wealth. The killings became known as the Osage Reign of Terror and resulted in a two-and-a-half-year investigation by the U.S. Justice Department's Bureau of Investigation, the forerunner of today's F.B.I.

When the Osage tribe purchased their reservation from the Cherokees in 1872, no one suspected that vast reserves of black gold lay beneath the surface. The discovery of oil was to prove a mixed blessing for the Osage. After oil was discovered in the 1890s, further exploration resulted in some major strikes. By 1906, over five million barrels were being produced annually.

The 2,229 members of the Osage tribe, called original allottees, had each received 658 acres of land in 1906. All mineral rights, however, were held in common by the tribe. Each Osage held a headright, which was an equal share in all mineral income. The royalties paid on each barrel of oil produced, plus bonuses paid to lease the land to drill upon, soon made the Osages wealthy.

There were more Pierce-Arrows in the Osage Nation than any other place in the country. The story about an Osage's car breaking down or having a flat and being abandoned was not an exaggeration. The Osage could easily afford to replace a troublesome vehicle with a new one. The Osage payments peaked at over $30 million for the year 1923. By 1925, the average Osage family was receiving over $65,000 per year. As the older members of the tribe died, their heirs inherited not only their estates, but their headrights as well.

Oilmen like Phillips, Sinclair, and Getty built enormous fortunes producing oil in the Osage Nation. There was fierce competition to acquire the oil leases giving the companies the right to drill on the 160-acre tracts of land. Often the auctions saw bids top one million dollars just for the right to drill. The tree on the Osage Agency grounds where Colonel E. E. Walters conducted these outdoor auctions became known as the "Million Dollar Elm."

As the oil royalties poured in, a new invasion of treacherous whites accompanied the wealth. Congress decreed that allotment payments would be made only to "competent" tribal members to safeguard against them squandering their money. Osages whose degree of Indian blood was 50 percent or greater had to demonstrate competency, or they would be "restricted." The court would appoint a "guardian" who placed their Osage "ward" on an allowance and a budget to prevent unwise use of their wealth.

Like may well-intentioned government interventions, this practice enabled the Osage Reign of Terror. Many of the guardians turned out to be unscrupulous lawyers (of whom there were eighty in the small town of Pawhuska) who robbed their wards blind.

Exactly how many Osage were murdered will probably never be known. Homicides were made to look like accidents and suicides. Poisonings with strychnine-laced whiskey followed by overdoes of injectable morphine was a favored method. Death certificates were falsified. Estimates of those murdered ranged from twenty-four to sixty, but some have speculated over a hundred.

The crimes took on a more violent tone when wealthy Osage County rancher William K. Hale became involved. Hale did not have an Indian wife, but his nephew Earnest did. It didn't take Hale long to figure out that if the relatives of Earnest's Osage wife, Mollie, were disposed of, she would inherit their fortunes and headrights. When Mollie's relatives began dying off at an alarming rate under unnatural circumstances, suspicions became aroused.

Mollie's two sisters, Anna Brown and Rita Smith, were murdered, and her mother, Lizzie Q, died under suspicious circumstances. Lizzie Q had inherited several headrights, which passed on to Mollie when she died. Rumors abounded that Hale and Earnest Burkhart were behind the killings.

Anna Brown's body was discovered on May 28, 1921, in a ravine near the Fairfax Country Club. A witness, Katharine Cole-Morrison, later testified that Earnest Burkhart's brother Byron and his friend Kelsie Morrison had gotten Anna drunk and killed her. Henry Roan, Mollie Burkhart's first husband, was next found dead and frozen in his car on February 6, 1923. He had been shot in the head like Anna Brown. W. K. Hale had taken out a $25,000 insurance policy on Roan's life. Following Roan's death, the insurance company that held the policy, Capital Life Insurance Company, hired Wiley Haines to investigate the murder. Haines shared his findings with the Bureau men working on the case, who expressed their appreciation: "We are also keeping in touch with Wiley Haines who has been an officer in this section for thirty years and has many old friends here.... He is reliable and an old-time friend of Agent Weiss and will give us all information and assistance possible."[1] Haines also interviewed other witnesses for the Bureau.

Then on March 13, 1923, the town of Fairfax was rocked with the most spectacular of all the murders. At 3 A.M. the W. E. Smith residence was bombed, killing W. E. Smith, his wife, Rita Smith, who was also the sister of Mollie Burkhart, and their white servant girl, seventeen-year-old Nettie Brookshire.

W. E. Smith had accused Hale of being behind Anna Brown's murder, so Hale had reason to want him dead. An exhaustive investigation by the Bureau resulted in Hale and Ramsey finally being charged with Roan's murder. Since Roan was murdered on restricted land, the case fell under federal jurisdiction. The State of Oklahoma followed suit, charging Earnest Burkhart as co-conspirator in the bombing death of W. E. and Rita Smith and their housekeeper. A chemist from Oklahoma A&M College determined that nitroglycerin was used in blowing up the house.

Because of Hale's wealth and influence, the probability of obtaining a conviction was low. Witnesses could not be found to testify because of their fear of Hale. The first trial of Hale and Ramsey ended in a hung jury. The jury was dismissed on August 25, 1926, after nearly fifty hours of deliberation. It was rumored that the jury had been bribed. A letter dated August 20, 1926, from Wiley Haines to sons John and Virgil stated, "Just got back from Guthrie yester-day, 24 days in the Hale-Ramsey trial."[2]

National attention was captured as the bloody tale unfolded in the press. The *New York Evening World* described, "The efforts of an evidently well-organized band, diabolic in its ruthlessness, to destroy with bullet, poison and bomb the heirs to the oil-rich Osage Indians."[3] The *World* continued, "But even lurid fiction pales beside the story of the Osage murders."[3] Writer Bill Burchardt later wrote, "The nation was astonished, shocked and secretly delighted, to find a last outpost of the Old West still alive, 'raising hell and putting a chunk under it.' It made for avid reading, boosted newspaper circula-tion, and brought forth howls of condemnation from the righteous."[4]

The Hale and Ramsey case was retried in Oklahoma City on October 29, 1926. Luther Bishop, with Oklahoma's State Bureau of Investigation, got the idea of having convicted bank robber Blackie Thompson released from the penitentiary to testify under immunity in the Hale case. Thompson testified that Hale had offered him $1,000 and a new Buick to blow up the Smith home. Thompson refused.

Ernest Burkhart finally confessed that he procured the murder-ers of the Smiths. At Hale's instructions, Earnest approached John Ramsey, who contacted Henry Grammar (world champion roper and bootlegger), Al Spencer (bank and train robber), and Curly Johnson (smalltime crook). All of them turned the job down. A deal was eventually made with Ace Kirby, who blew up the house with nitroglycerin.

Kirby was subsequently killed in an attempted store robbery in June of 1923. Grammar was killed in a motor vehicle accident in June of 1923, and Curly Johnson died after drinking poisoned whiskey. Al Spencer was shot to death by Luther Bishop and other officers in September of 1923. Bishop was then murdered in his sleep at his home on December 6, 1926.

Earnest Burkhart further testified that Hale had hired Ramsey to kill Henry Roan for $500 and a new Ford. Hale denied everything at the trial and insisted he had no reason to want Roan killed (despite the $25,000 insurance policy, which he claimed secured a debt).

In this second trial, the jury came back with a guilty verdict. Hale, Ramsey, and Burkhart all received sentences for life impris-onment at Leavenworth Federal Penitentiary. Hale appealed, was retried in 1929, and again was found guilty. Ramsey also appealed, and during his retrial revealed why Roan was killed. Ramsey claimed that Mollie Burkhart had decided to divorce Earnest and re-marry Henry Roan, her first husband. If Mollie had left Earnest, he would have lost all claim to his wife's inherited wealth. Despite this new information, Ramsey was again found guilty.

At least twenty Osage murders were never solved. An unknown number of whites also were killed in connection with the Osage murders. Luther Bishop may have been one, and W. W. Vaughn was likely another. The Bureau of Investigation learned that Hale and Burkhart took George Big Heart, an Osage dying from poisoned whiskey, by train to the State Hospital in Oklahoma City. Big Heart had previously signed over the management of his headright to Hale. Big Heart sent for his attorney, W. W. Vaughn, from Pawhuska. After Big Heart died, Vaughn took the night train to Pawhuska. He never arrived. The next day his body was found on the railroad right-of-way in Osage County. He had been shot in the head.[5]

After two and a half years of inquiry by the Bureau of Investigation, evidence had been obtained against twenty-four persons. After interviewing hundreds of people, the F.B.I.'s file on the Osage murders contained 3,274 pages. But the cases were not a priority for the F.B.I.'s new director, J. Edgar Hoover.

Hoover was more interested in pursuing high-profile gangsters like John Dillinger than in solving Indian murders. Putting only three men behind bars was certainly a poor showing for the new Bureau of Investigation. But the convictions did help end the bloodiest phase of the Osage Reign of Terror.

Hale was imprisoned eleven years before being paroled on July 31, 1947, over the protests of the Osage National Council. Ramsey was also paroled four months later. Burkhart, however, remained in prison another twelve years. He was finally released from the penitentiary in McAlester in October 1959.

Burkhart remained a bitter man, claiming that federal agents had promised he'd never serve a day in prison for his cooperation in providing evidence against Hale and Ramsey.

CHAPTER XVI

LAST CAMPAIGN

As the last of the outlaw gangs were broken up after the turn of the century, Wiley Haines continued to serve in various capacities as an officer. In 1913 he received an appointment from the U.S. Commissioner of Indian Affairs as a special officer in suppressing the liquor traffic. Haines' years of arresting bootleggers in the Osage made him an expert when Prohibition became the law of the land.

In 1914 Wiley made an unsuccessful run for sheriff of Osage County. He also served as a special consultant for the Texas Rangers to help suppress liquor trafficking. In 1927 Governor Henry S. Johnston named Haines a special investigator for liquor trafficking in Oklahoma.

One month before his sixty-eighth birthday, Haines showed no signs of slackening his pace. He was waging a second vigorous campaign for the Democratic nomination for sheriff of Osage County. His campaign slogan was, "I think a snitch is a copperhead snake— he will bite you if he can." A photo taken for the sheriff's race showed that the aging lawman still looked every inch the frontier marshal.

But it was 1928, and times had changed. Haines had been born before the outbreak of the Civil War, and in just eleven years World War II would commence. He lost out on the nomination for sheriff, but remained on as a deputy.

On September 24, 1928, Haines was in Pawhuska on business

and climbed the sixty-six steps that led from Kihekah Street to the top of the hill where the courthouse was located. At the door of the county clerk's office, he collapsed in the arms of Deputy Sheriff Ed Clewein. In a matter of minutes the lawman was dead, felled by a heart attack.

Word rapidly spread of Haines' death, and condolences poured in from around the state. On September 28, 1928, funeral services were held at the First Baptist Church in Hominy. The church was packed with relatives, friends, and associates who had come to pay their last respects. The service was conducted by Reverend R. E. Cornelius, and the eulogy was given by Judge Hugh Jones. The interment was under the direction of the Masonic Lodge, for Haines had been a life member of Consistory #1 in Guthrie. The pallbearers included J. E. Martin, Charlie Franks, John L. Freeman, George M. Treadway, W. S. Morrow, and J.L. Flint.

Haines' funeral was believed to be the largest ever held in Hominy. He was buried in the first plot in the Hominy City Cemetery. The inscription on his tombstone succinctly sums up Haines' life: "An Honest Man's the Noblest Work of God."

EPILOGUE

Along a lonely stretch of State Highway 99, between the small Osage County towns of Wynona and Pawhuska, stands a six-foot granite marker. The marker commemorates the famous gun battle between Haines, Bennett, and Majors, and the Martin gang. The solitary monument symbolizes the life of Wiley Haines, who so often was the sole representative of law and order.

On October 28, 1995, the dedication of the historical marker was held. It was a small, quiet ceremony of about 100 ancestors, historians, officials, and interested onlookers. The governor and a U.S. senator were invited but did not attend the event. However, the U.S. marshal for the northern district of Oklahoma, Jim Hughes, the chief deputy marshal, Robin Fagala, and other lawmen were in attendance. This would have pleased Haines, as he held his fellow officers in the highest esteem.

It is difficult to describe the bond between frontier marshals, but it certainly transcended the ties of ordinary friendship. Such a bond existed between Wiley Haines and men like Charles Colcord, Frank Canton, and Warren Bennett. In Luther Hill's *History of the State of Oklahoma*, the relationship between Colcord and Haines was described thus: "and the two have ever since remained the warmest of friends, the dangers they underwent in contending with the criminal and lawless elements of those days cementing a bond of attachment typical of comrades in frontier life."[1]

The *Tulsa World* wrote an editorial upon Wiley's death with the poignant title "The Advance Guard Recedes." With the passing away of lawmen like Wiley, an era of American frontier history was passing as well:

> To the newer generation it is inconceivable that the situation which Haines and his comrades handled ever existed in the vicinity of Tulsa. Except as to location, this is a totally different region. It is hardly possible to realize that Haines, who died in his sixties, was a mature man when he tracked the horrible James gang through the Osage wilds; when he scouted for weeks at a time after the Daltons; when he shot numerous members of the Martin gang and was shot down by them. His whole official career, which conservatively written, might be considered dime novel stuff, was within a hundred miles of Tulsa. The country was wild then and for every person then living in the six-shooter bailiwick there are now many hundreds.
>
> There was in the time of Haines, Bud Ledbetter and Frank Canton no elaborate law organization. An officer was then literally the law and nothing but his judgment and his trigger finger stood between him and extermination. He had nowhere to pass the buck, no alibi, no reinforcements. It was often a case of a lone man against a pack of cunning devils long used to the brush and the cave. These men of law had no brass bands, typewriter or press agents and they had to be deadly as rattlesnakes.
>
> Haines, like most of the real officers of his time, was rather modest and unpretentious. Practically none of the old-time officers—with the exception of Heck Thomas—had the courtly manner, the dramatic look or the towering presence. They were the forerunners of our civilization and the job was a grim one. They were just as far from the movie type of gun-fighter as possible. They were direct representatives of the United States and they acted directly.
>
> The passing of these unromantic men constitutes the passing of a romantic era. It was a rough and ugly era, but in the light of that which came after, it was heroic and exciting.[2]

ENDNOTES

Chapter I
1. *Hominy News*, September 26, 1928.
2. Croy, Homer. *Trigger Marshal: The Story of Chris Madsen*. New York: Duell, Sloan, and Pearce, 1958.
3. *Hominy News*, September, 1928.

Chapter II
1. Settle, William. *Jesse James Was His Name*. Lincoln: University of Nebraska Press, 1966.
2. Haines, William Francis, personal papers.
3. "Alton's Disaster in War Between States," undated clipping form the *Alton Telegraph*, Hayner Public Library, Alton, Illinois.
4. *Hominy News*, undated clipping.
5. Haines, John Wesley. *Richard Haines and His Descendants*. Boyce, Virginia: Carr Publishing Co., 1961.
6. Haines, John W. *The History of the Polk County Baptist Association*. Bolivar, Missouri: The Bolivar Herald, 1897.

Chapter III
1. *Hominy News*, September 26, 1928.
2. Haines, John W. Letter to Wiley Haines, June 20, 1888.

Chapter IV
1. Walker, Dr. Delos. *The Daily Oklahoman*, April 22, 1909.
2. Marshall, James. *Santa Fe: The Railroad That Built an Empire*. New York: Random House, 1945.
3. White, Robe Carl. "Experiences at the Opening of Oklahoma 1889." *Chronicles of Oklahoma*, vol. XXVII, no. 1 (Spring 1949).

4. McMartin, D. F. *Thirty Years in Hell.* Topeka: Copper Printing, 1921.
5. Shirley, Glenn. *West of Hell's Fringe.* Norman: University of Oklahoma Press, 1978.
6. Personal communication from Joe D. Haines, Sr.
7. Colcord, Charles F. *Autobiography of Charles Francis Colcord.* N.p.: Privately printed by C.C. Helmerich, 1970.
8. Shirley, Glenn. *West of Hell's Fringe.*
9. *Guthrie Daily News,* September 20, 1893.
10. Shirley Glenn. *Guardian of the Law.* Austin: Eakin Press, 1988.
11. Ibid.
12. Ibid.
13. Ibid.

Chapter V
1. *Stillwater Gazette,* undated clipping.
2. Colcord, Charles F. *Autobiography of Charles Francis Colcord.* N.p.: Privately published by C.C. Helmerich, 1970.
3. Canton, Frank. *Frontier Trails: The Autobiography of Frank N. Canton.* Boston: Houghton Mifflin Co., 1930.
4. Colcord, Charles F. *Autobiography of Charles Francis Colcord.*
5. Canton, Frank. *Frontier Trails.*
6. Shirley, Glenn. *West of Hell's Fringe.* Norman: University of Oklahoma Press, 1978.

Chapter VI
1. Canton, Frank. *Frontier Trails: The Autobiography of Frank N. Canton.* Boston: Houghton Mifflin Co., 1930.
2. Colcord, Charles F. *Autobiography of Charles Francis Colcord.* N.p.: Privately printed by C.C. Helmerich, 1970.
3. Canton, Frank. *Frontier Trails.*
4. Ibid.
5. Nix, Edward D. *Oklahombres, Particularly the Wilder Ones.* St. Louis: Eden Publishing House, 1929.
6. DeArment, Robert K. *Alias Frank Canton.* Norman: University of Oklahoma Press, 1996.
7. Croy, Homer. *Trigger Marshal: The Story of Chris Madsen.* New York: Duell, Sloan, and Pearce, 1958.
8. Samuleson, Nancy. *Shoot From the Lip.* Eastford, CT: Shooting Star Press, 1998.
9. Ibid.

Chapter VII
1. *Hominy News,* undated clipping.
2. Ibid.

3. *Osage Journal,* May 16, 1901.
4. *Hominy News,* undated clipping.

Chapter VIII

1. *Hominy News,* August 18 and 25, 1960.
2. Ibid., September 1928.
3. *Osage Journal,* January 3, 1901.
4. U.S. Indian Agent's Annual Report.
5. *Pawhuska Journal Capital,* May 4, 1905.
6. U.S. Indian Agent's Annual Report, 1916.
7. Ibid.
8. Ibid.
9. Haines, Wiley G. Daily logbook, 1899–1900.

Chapter IX

1. Shirley, Glenn. *They Outrobbed Them All.* Stillwater, Okla.: Barbed Wire Press, 1992.
2. Ibid.
3. Ibid.
4. Ibid.
5. Ibid.

Chapter X

1. *Bartlesville Weekly Examiner,* August 15, 1903.
2. Haines, Joe D., Jr. "A Sensational Hold-Up." *True West,* January 1984.
3. *Bartlesville Weekly Examiner,* August 15, 1903.

Chapter XI

1. Shirley, Glenn. *They Outrobbed Them All.* Stillwater, Okla.: Barbed Wire Press, 1992.
2. *Oklahoma City Times,* July 25, 1921.
3. Personal communication from Kenneth Haines.
4. *Guthrie Daily Leader,* March 6–7, 1903.
5. Ibid.
6. Ibid.
7. Ibid.
8. Ibid.
9. *Oklahoma State Capital,* March 7–8, 1903.
10. Letter from U.S.D.M. Warren Bennett to Marshal Fossett.
11. Letter from Fossett to Bennett.
12. *The Daily Oklahoman,* January 28, 1921.
13. Ibid.
14. Ibid.

Chapter XII
1. *Osage Journal,* July 18, 1901.
2. Nix, Edward D. *Oklahombres, Particularly the Wilder Ones.* St. Louis: Eden Publishing House, 1929.
3. Ibid.

Chapter XIII
1. *Pawhuska Journal Capitol,* undated clipping.
2. *Hominy News,* undated clipping.
3. *Pawhuska Journal Capitol,* undated clipping.
4. *Foraker Tribune,* undated clipping.

Chapter XIV
1. Shirley, Glenn. *Guardian of the Law.* Austin: Eakin Press, 1988.
2. Ibid.
3. Ibid.
4. Jackson, Robert B. *The Remarkable Ride of the Abernathy Boys.* New York: Walck, 1967.
5. Ibid.

Chapter XV
1. Letter from F.B.I. files.
2. Personal letter from Wiley to sons, John and Virgil, August 20, 1926.
3. *New York Evening World,* undated clipping.
4. Burckhart, Bill. *Oklahoma Chronicles.*
5. Frank, Kenny. *The Osage Oil Boom.* Oklahoma City: Oklahoma Heritage Assoc., 1989.

Epilogue
1. Hill, Luther. *A History of the State of Oklahoma.,* vol. II. Chicago: Lewis Publishing Company, 1909.
2. *Tulsa World,* September 28, 1928.

BIBLIOGRAPHY

Books

Canton, Frank M. *Frontier Trails: The Autobiography of Frank M. Canton.* Boston: Houghton Mifflin Co., 1930.

Colcord, Charles Francis. *Autobiography of Charles Francis Colcord.* N.p.: Privately printed by C.C. Helmerich.

Croy, Homer. *Trigger Marshal: The Story of Chris Madsen.* New York: Duell, Sloan, and Pearce, 1958.

DeArment, Robert K. *Alias Frank Canton.* Norman: University of Oklahoma Press, 1996.

Franks, Kenny A. *The Osage Oil Boom.* Oklahoma City: Oklahoma Heritage Association, 1989.

Gibson, A. M. *Oklahoma, a History of Five Centuries.* Norman; Harlow Publishing Corp., 1965.

Haines, John W. *The History of the Polk County Baptist Association.* Bolivar, Missouri: The Bolivar Herald, 1897.

———. *Richard Haines and his Descendants.* Boyce, Virginia: Carr Publishing Co., 1961.

Hill, Luther B. *A History of the State of Oklahoma,* vol. II. Chicago: Lewis Publishing Company, 1909.

Jackson, Robert B. *The Remarkable Ride of the Abernathy Boys.* New York: Walck, 1967.

Lamb, Arthur. *Tragedies of the Osage Hills.* Pawhuska, Okla: Osage Printery, 1935.

McCauliffe, Dennis. *The Deaths of Sybil Bolton.* New York: Random House, 1994.

Nix, E. D. *Oklahombres, Particularly the Wilder Ones.* St. Louis: Eden Publishing House, 1929.

Prassel, Frank R. *The Western Peace Officer.* Norman: University of Oklahoma Press, 1972.

Samuelson, Nancy. *Shoot From the Lip.* Eastford, Conn.: Shooting Star Press, 1998.

Settle, William. *Jesse James Was His Name.* Lincoln: University of Nebraska Press, 1977.

Shirley, Glenn. *Guardian of the Law: The Life and Times of William Matthew Tilghman.* Austin, Tex.: Eakin Press, 1988.

———. *Heck Thomas, Frontier Marshal.* Norman: University of Oklahoma Press, 1981.

———. *West of Hell's Fringe.* Norman: University of Oklahoma Press, 1978.

———. *They Outrobbed Them All.* Stillwater, Okla: Barbed Wire Press, 1992.

Speer, Bonnie. *Portrait of a Lawman.* Norman: Reliance Press, 1996.

Unpublished Materials

Wiley Haines personal papers. Collection of Joe D. Haines, Sr., Osage County, Oklahoma.

Newspapers

Bartlesville Weekly Examiner, August 15, 1903.

Daily Oklahoman, April 22, 1909, January 28, 1921.

Guthrie Daily Leader, March 6, 7, 1903.

Guthrie Daily News, September 20, 1893.

Hominy News, September 26, 1928; August 18, 25, 1960.

Oklahoma City Times, July 25, 1921.

Oklahoma State Capitol, March 7, 8, 1903.

Osage Journal, January 3, 1901; May 16, 1901; July 18, 1901.

Pawhuska Journal Capitol, undated clippings.

Stillwater Gazette, undated clippings.

Tulsa World, September 28, 1928.

Articles

Burchardt, Bill. "Osage Oil." *Chronicles of Oklahoma* 61 (1963): 264.

Haines, Joe D., Jr. "The Log of a Frontier Marshal." *Chronicles of Oklahoma* 59 (1981–82): 295–303.

———. "A Sensational Hold-Up." *True West* (January 1984).

White, Robe Carl. "Experiences at the Opening of Oklahoma 1889." *Chronicles of Oklahoma* 1 (Spring 1949).

Government Documents

State of Oklahoma v. William K. Hale, John Ramsey, Earnest Burkhart: Osage County District Court.

Federal Bureau of Investigation files pertaining to the Osage murders.

ACKNOWLEDGMENTS

The world will always need heroes and those who chronicle their lives. Wiley Haines has been a personal hero since my childhood. One of my goals was to tell his story so that my sons, Cy, Avery, Bret, and Chase, and others would know of my great-grandfather. Over the past fifteen years, as I gathered information on the life and times of Wiley Haines, I occasionally speculated about how I would handle any negative material. I wanted to write an objective and credible account, but this was my ancestor and my hero. Remarkably, the dilemma never arose. Years of research confirmed Wiley's impeccable reputation, both personally and professionally.

I have had a great deal of help in putting this story together, especially from my parents, Joe and Shirley Haines. I also want to thank all the relatives who came forward with information and photographs.

INDEX

scribed, vii-viii; and Oklahoma land run, 13-14, 15, 16; and Osage Indians, vii-viii, 19; and Osage Nation, 32-34; and "Osage Reign of Terror," 72-76; and outlaws, 20-25, 26-31; and Martin gang, 44-48, 49-51, 52-59; reports by, 2, 39-43; becomes U.S. Deputy Marshal, 17; wounded, 54-57

Haines, Wiley, Jr. (child of Wiley and Sarah), 34

Haines, William Francis, 6

Hale, William K., 73, 74

Hall, James, 41

Harlow, Jack, 40, 41

Harris, D. H., 43

Harrison, Benjamin, 12

Hell's Half Acre, 18

Hewitt, J. N., 40

Heynes, Simeon, 7-8

Hickok, Wild Bill, viii, 1

Hill, Luther, 79

History of the State of Oklahoma (book), viii, 79

Holt, Bill, 47

Hominy, Oklahoma, 33

Hoover, J. Edgar, 76

Horner, Joe, 28, 29

Hough, Emerson, 9

Hughes, Jim, 79

Hull, Charles, 44-45

Hull, Mrs., 45

I

Indian Appropriation Bill, 12

Indian Territory, formation of, 1; lawlessness in, vii, 1-2

Ingalls, Oklahoma, 20-21, 22

Ingram, Alex, 40

J

Jackson, Robert B., 71

Jacobson, Marshal, 56

James, Frank, 20

James gang, 80

James, Jesse, 20, 54

James-Younger gang, 20

Johnson, Curly, 75

Johnston, Henry S., 19, 77

Jones, Hugh, 78

Jones, John P., 67

K

Kansas Territory, 4

Kapp, Rolla, 60-61

Keeler, Fred, 49, 50

Kelly, Frank, 64, 65

Kendrick, Dan, 41

King, Perry, 42

Kirby, Ace, 75

Knox, James G., 67

L

Labdell, J., 40

Lake, Frank, 17, 28, 29

Lawrence, Maggie, 41

Lawson, George, 24

Ledbetter, Bud, viii, 31, 80

Leonard, W. D., 42, 43

Lincoln, Abraham, 4, 5

Linn, Wm., 41

liquor, 38, 77

Logan, John, 40

Long, Dr., 11

Lookout, Fred, 36

Lynch, Joseph, 63

lynching, 63-66

Lyon, Nathaniel, 5, 6

M

MacMartin, D. F., 14-15

Madsen, Chris, 2, 30-31, 58, 67

Majors, Henry, 54, 57, 58, 59

Mangas Colorado (chief), 10

Martin brothers, 25

Martin gang, 44-48, 49-51, 52-59, 79, 80

ABOUT THE AUTHOR

J. D. Haines traveled and lived throughout the world while growing up, due to his father's career in the oil industry. He attended preparatory school at Notre Dame International School for Boys, Rome, Italy. He graduated from Oklahoma State University with a B.S. in science in 1977 and the University of Oklahoma College of Medicine with an M.D. in 1981. Haines is board-certified in family medicine, has extensive experience in emergency medicine, and is a Fellow of the American College of Sports Medicine. He has practiced medicine in Oklahoma for twenty years and is currently owner of Stillwater Family Medicine and Urgent Care Center in Stillwater, Oklahoma. Haines is a clinical associate professor of family and preventative medicine at the University of Oklahoma.

Haines is a graduate of the U.S. Army Combat Casualty Care Course and is currently a lieutenant commander in the U.S. Naval Reserves. He is assigned to a surgical unit with the United States Marine Corps. Haines was called to active duty with the U.S. Air Force during Desert Storm.

Haines is the author of more than a hundred articles published in a variety of magazines and professional journals. He served for four years as a medical editor for *Postgraduate Medicine.* In addition to *Wiley Haines: Frontier U.S. Deputy Marshal,* Haines has several other books in press, including a book of memoirs, *There Ain't No U-Haul Behind That Hearse,* a young-adult novel, *Flight of the*

Eagle, a collection of Civil War stories, *Deo Vindice*, and a collection of Old West history, *Wild and Woolly*.

Haines and his wife, Pam, have four sons, Cy, Avery, Bret, and Chase. Cy and Avery will be midshipmen at the United States Naval Academy in 2002.

www.ingramcontent.com/pod-product-compliance
Lightning Source LLC
Chambersburg PA
CBHW020202090426
42734CB00008B/913